THREE

The three plays published here represent three landmarks in the journey from traditional to modern theatre in France. All three playwrights rebelled against nineteenth-century conventions but each in a very different manner. Maurice Maeterlinck, with *The Blind* (1890), sought escape in a mystical dream-world of symbolism; but he also incorporated radical new ideas which inspired generations of playwrights and directors. Alfred Jarry's rebellion was much more violent. His *Ubu the King* (1896) is an irreverent, outrageous parody of everything his predecessors held dear: not only moral values but also sustained character portrayal, coherent plot, and consistent language. Apollinaire's play *The Mammaries of Tiresias* (1917) is deliberately forward-looking. He explicitly rejects tradition, and sets out to write something different and new. The result is a zany, witty farce, but with a strong imaginative quality, as befits a poet. Apollinaire invented the word 'surrealism' to describe his play—his Preface, which constitutes the first manifesto of surrealism, is published here. After *Tiresias*, and Apollinaire's untimely death, he became acknowledged as the father of surrealism—but all three plays each in its own way, contain elements of the surreal.

MAYA SLATER is Senior Lecturer in French at Queen Mary and Westfield College, London. She is the author of *Humour in the Works of Proust* (OUP, 1979). In 1995, she edited La Fontaine, *Selected Fables*, translated by Christopher Wood (OUP World's Classics), and in 1996, *Actes du colloque La Fontaine de Londres* (Papers in Seventeenth-Century French Literature; Tübingen). She has given lectures and papers on literature and theatre in four continents, and published many articles on these subjects. She has also written theatre reviews. She has recently completed a book, *The Craft of La Fontaine*.

THE WORLD'S CLASSICS

Three Pre-Surrealist Plays

The Blind
(Les Aveugles)

Ubu the King
(Ubu roi)

The Mammaries of Tiresias
(Les Mamelles de Tirésias)

Translated with an Introduction and Notes by
MAYA SLATER

Oxford   New York

OXFORD UNIVERSITY PRESS

Oxford University Press, Great Clarendon Street, Oxford OX2 6DP

Oxford New York

Athens Auckland Bangkok Bogota Bombay Buenos Aires
Calcutta Cape Town Dar es Salaam Delhi Florence Hong Kong
Istanbul Karachi Kuala Lumpur Madras Madrid Melbourne
Mexico City Nairobi Paris Singapore Taipei Tokyo Toronto Warsaw

and associated companies in
Berlin Ibadan

Oxford is a trade mark of Oxford University Press

© Maya Slater 1997

First published as a World's Classics paperback 1997

British Library Cataloguing in Publication Data
Data available

Library of Congress Cataloging in Publication Data
Three pre-surrealist plays/translated and edited with an introduction by Maya Slater.
(World's classics)
Includes bibliographical references.
Contents: The blind / by Maurice Maeterlinck—Ubu the king / by Alfred Jarry—The mammaries
of Tiresias / by Guillaume Apollinaire.
1. French drama–20th century–Translations into English. I. Slater, Maya. II. Maeterlinck,
Maurice, 1862–1949. Aveugles. English. III. Jarry, Alfred, 1873–1907. Ubu roi. English.
IV. Apollinaire, Guillaume, 1880–1918. Mamelles de Tirésias. English. V. Title: Blind.
VI. Title: Ubu the king. VII. Title: Mammaries of Tiresias. VIII. Series.
PQ1240.E5T63 1998   842'.808–dc21   96–52367
ISBN 0–19–283217–4 (pb)

3 5 7 9 10 8 6 4 2

Printed in Great Britain by
Caledonian International Book Manufacturing Ltd.
Glasgow

CONTENTS

Acknowledgements   vii

Introduction   ix

Note on the Translation   xliii

Select Bibliography   xlviii

A Chronology of Maurice Maeterlinck   li

A Chronology of Alfred Jarry   lv

A Chronology of Guillaume Apollinaire   lviii

THE BLIND by Maurice Maeterlinck   1

UBU THE KING by Alfred Jarry   49

THE MAMMARIES OF TIRESIAS
  by Guillaume Apollinaire   151

Explanatory Notes   208

ACKNOWLEDGEMENTS

THANKS are due to James Redmond for reading the Introduction, and providing many valuable suggestions. By asking me to translate *Ubu roi* for a new production, he was the original inspiration for this book. I am also indebted to Elza Adamowicz for reading the Introduction, and making many helpful comments. Finally, I should like to thank my husband for his unfailing help and support.

M.S.

and copulating, and depicts colourful characters like La Mère Caca (old Ma Crap), who urinates but charges with her own excrement. Perhaps it was fortunate for the theatre that Zola himself was not a skilled playwright. His attempts to drama- tise some of his novels met with limited success, and his nove-

INTRODUCTION

THESE three plays represent three acts of rebellion. The three playwrights knew each other personally, and had ambivalent feelings about each other's work. But in one respect they were united—in their need to reject their common dramatic heritage.

The theatre of late nineteenth-century Paris laboured under a stifling burden of tradition. The century had witnessed a long series of conventional plays, melodramas for serious audiences, and farces for the more light-hearted. It must have seemed as if there was nothing more to theatre than tragically bereaved young ladies, their eyes raised heavenwards, often dressed in becoming period costume. In addition, playwrights such as the younger Dumas used their tragic heroines to teach an edifying lesson. Their comic counterparts were Feydeau's pert Paris- iennes, each with her secret lover lurking in her wardrobe.

As a reaction to these stultifyingly stereotyped pieces, André Antoine founded his Théâtre libre (Free Theatre) in 1887. Antoine was an enthusiastic disciple of the novelist Emile Zola and the Naturalist movement. Since Balzac, much earlier in the century, novelists had come to believe that life was not there to be prettified into such stereotypes. Instead, it should be shown in its true colours. With Zola, this tendency towards realism crystallized into a literary movement. One has only to read a Zola novel to see the extent to which he chooses to emphasize the sordid realities of life. He prefers to describe the poorer strata of society, and far from shrinking from crude details, seems to revel in them. In his novel *La Terre* (*The Earth*), for instance, Zola treats us to peasants farting, cursing, and copulating, and depicts colourful characters like La Mère Caca (Old Ma Crap), who manures her cabbages with her own excrement. Perhaps it was fortunate for the theatre that Zola himself was not a talented playwright. His attempts to dramatize some of his novels met with limited success, and his movement failed to find dramatic writers of sufficient stature to match their novelist counterparts. Antoine, however, adopted the tenets of Naturalism with gusto. In one play, *Les Bouchers* (*The Butchers*, 1888) he went so far as to hang real animal carcasses on the stage. After the first few days of the run, the atmosphere in the theatre became somewhat too naturalistic for comfort.

The young Belgian playwright, Maurice Maeterlinck, came to the theatre with very different ideas from those of the traditional nineteenth-century playwrights and their successors the Naturalists. Arriving in Paris, he initially joined Antoine, then followed the young directors Paul Fort and Aurélien Lugné-Poe when they broke with the Théâtre libre to found their own companies: Fort's Théâtre d'art and Lugné-Poe's Théâtre de l'Œuvre.

Maeterlinck was Fort's first great success as an innovator, and his plays can without doubt be seen as a reaction against nineteenth-century theatre. He discards the historical dramas and drawing-room comedies alike. Equally, he rejects naturalism with its adoption of the crude details of ordinary life as subjects for theatre. Instead, he focuses on a different tradition, poetry. Maeterlinck's drama has strong links with the symbolist poetry of the time; he was a disciple and admirer of Villiers de l'Isle Adam and of Mallarmé. However, he saw himself very much as a playwright, and wrote his plays for performance, not reading. His predilection is for mysticism and metaphysics. He is drawn to myth and legend. He makes no attempt to situate his characters—to give them roots in what seems like recognizable reality. If they seem mysterious and even incomprehensible, so much the better. Similarly, the problems that provide the intrigue of the plays are visibly human dilemmas, but stripped of their contemporary trappings. He will present, as abstract phenomena, a child's longing for its family (*The Blue Bird*) or a woman's love for a man (*Pelleas and Melisande*). But the most striking emotion in Maeterlinck is an unfocused sense of distress and unease, an inexplicable, nightmarish fear, which links these dramas to the world of dreams. Maeterlinck's rebellion against nineteenth-century theatre leads him off down the solitary path of the mystical seer, the Tiresias of the turn of the century.

Jarry was Maeterlinck's contemporary, and like him, was associated with Lugné-Poe. But whereas *The Blind* was proudly presented as a talented young playwright's latest work, *Ubu the King* owed its only two performances during his lifetime to the machinations of its author. Jarry had an administrative post at Lugné-Poe's Théâtre de l'Œuvre and tricked the bemused theatre director into putting on the play, organizing the whole event himself behind the scenes. The scandalous events surrounding this first performance, which will be described later, are typical of this iconoclastic rebel, whose revolt against his predecessors' theatre is much more flamboyant and violent than Maeterlinck's. Whereas the young Belgian goes off at a tangent, abandoning theatre convention to follow his own original path, Jarry chooses to cock a snook at everything that the previous generation stood for. The well-constructed melodramas of the nineteenth century, in Jarry's irreverent hands, are transformed into a clumsy, inconsequential muddle —characters drop out or die only to pop up again later. The conventions of French theatre, in which violent actions had been traditionally avoided on stage for centuries, are subverted in this drama of grotesquely exaggerated comic violence, in which crowds of victims are gleefully tortured and murdered before our eyes. 'Serious' subjects are no longer afforded any dignity—the king of Poland is noble and honourable, but he is routed in short order by a ludicrous buffoon.

But *Ubu* is equally a rejection of naturalism. Every detail of Jarry's work is deliberately far-fetched. Far from representing recognizable human types, the play's characters are supposed to be masked; the horses they ride to war are conceived as hobby-horses. The food they eat is not for human consumption (ratlet cutlets, juice of lavatory brush). They may or may not be mortal, since some of Ubu's murders are final, others not. This is not merely invention for its own sake—there is a definite feeling of irreverent mockery at the expense of accepted convention.

If we are to believe Apollinaire, he wrote *The Mammaries of Tiresias* only seven years after the first performance of *Ubu*, though it was not staged until some fifteen years later. At any rate, it is quite clear that he too is still preoccupied by the need to reject the two tendencies of nineteenth-century theatre. We know this because he tells us so himself. The Preface to *The Mammaries of Tiresias* is reproduced here in full because it constitutes the first manifesto of surrealism, and as such is an important document. (Apollinaire invented the actual term shortly before he wrote this Preface, when he used it in the programme notes for Cocteau's ballet *Parade*.) In this Preface, Apollinaire explicitly rejects both the conventional drama of the nineteenth century, and what he calls '*trompe-l'œil* naturalism'. He also takes a side-swipe at Maeterlinck and symbolist drama: 'there are no symbols in my play, which is quite transparent; but people are free to see in it all the symbols they wish, and to tease out a thousand meanings, as though it were a Delphic oracle.' Instead, he proposes a new kind of reality, created from the free-wheeling imagination of the author. As he puts it, 'I have chosen to give free rein to fantasy, my own way of interpreting nature'. The playwright should see important issues and look to the future, rather than trying to reproduce every sordid detail of the present. Indeed, Apollinaire sees the dramatist's function as that of a leader, helping mankind to a better world, and he expresses this in positively messianic terms: 'these men bring before our gaze new worlds to broaden our horizons, ever showing us more, and bringing us the joy and honour of ever advancing towards the most surprising discoveries.' Apollinaire was a friend and admirer of Jarry throughout the latter's short life. Nevertheless, implicitly, he is here rejecting Jarry's play just as he rejects Maeterlinck's: the wanton destructiveness and anarchy of *Ubu* is quite simply incompatible with his reforming zeal and serious underlying purpose. For in addition to his general desire to make of theatre a didactic genre, Apollinaire's Preface informs us that he also had a precise purpose in writing *The Mammaries of Tiresias*. The falling birth-rate in France during the early years of the twentieth century greatly worried him—and indeed, it was a cause for general concern. This play, he claims, represents his attempt to coax the French to mend their ways, and produce more children.

The definition of surrealism which Apollinaire includes in this Preface is almost incidental, subordinate in his mind to the play's immediate reforming purpose. He invented the word 'surrealism' in the context of his rejection of naturalism—he wanted to create a new kind of reality, more vivid than ordinary reality, hence 'sur-reality'. However, the off-beat weirdness which we associate with surrealism today was also somewhere at the back of his mind. He makes a revealing comment: 'When man resolved to imitate walking, he invented the wheel, which does not look like a leg. In doing this, he was practising surrealism without knowing it.' So as well as insisting that Frenchmen must reproduce, Apollinaire claimed he was setting out to stimulate the imagination of the audience. The first surrealist play was performed on 24 June 1917. For all Apollinaire's insistence on the play's reforming purpose in his Preface, written after the play was completed, it came across as an irreverent farce. As we shall see, it caused as much uproar as Jarry's iconoclastic masterpiece twenty years earlier.

These three plays were important in their time. But they are reproduced here not simply because of their historic interest, but because of their intrinsic value. Each of the three writers brought much that was new and interesting to the theatre.

The Blind was Maeterlinck's third play. It was first put on in December 1891, in a theatre sprayed with perfume to make it more atmospheric (an innovation occasionally emulated in the modern cinema with 'scratch and sniff' cards). It is a powerfully disturbing play. It presents a simple problem, which at the same time is endowed with a mysterious quality. The dilemma of the characters is apparent to the audience almost before any words are spoken, embodied in the strange figure we see as soon as the curtain rises, described by Maeterlinck in a detailed stage direction, which is simultaneously a colossal piece of dramatic irony:

Centre stage, and in the deepest shadows, is seated an ancient priest, wrapped in an ample black robe. His head and torso, tilted back a little and deathly still, are leaning against the trunk of an enormous hollow oak. His face, with its violet lips parted, is of a changeless waxen pallor. His expressionless staring eyes no longer look at the visible world this side of eternity...

In the original production, the priest was represented by a model, not a living actor.

Even if we have forgotten the play's title, we realize that the characters are all blind the moment they start to speak. The gripping quality of their predicament rests largely in its very simplicity. The blind depend on the priest to see them to safety; the audience can see the priest is dead, though the blind cannot; so the blind are without succour, although they do not know it. The centre stage is held by a dead man, and the other characters' fear of approaching death and their powerlessness to prevent it forms the central intrigue of the play.

The idea is so powerful and so sustained that Maeterlinck needs little in the way of artful writing to keep us gripped. Accordingly, the whole play is written in a style remarkable for its limpidity. The blind speak naïvely, like children: 'Aren't you scared in this place?' 'Which of us?' 'The whole lot of you!' 'Yes, yes, we're scared all right!' 'We've been scared for ages!' Their situation is stripped of any extraneous detail, so that we are not distracted from the central problem. This aspect was of great importance to Maeterlinck. For example, he did not want the priest's dog to appear on stage, but rather to be imagined by the audience (he was overruled by the director).

This pared-down quality adds an extra dimension to the play, and gives it much of its atmosphere. It is not that the characters' life-stories are omitted, or that we do not bother with them. Rather, there seem to be no details to give—the blind have come from nowhere in particular, they have no roots, they are lost souls. The passage in which they talk about their past is particularly elusive: 'So where are you from?' 'I couldn't say. How could I explain?—It's too far from here, way across the sea. I come from a big country... I could only show you by making signs; but we can't see any more... I've been a wanderer for too long... But I've seen the sun, and water and fire, and mountains and faces and strange flowers...' Their forgetfulness is unreal, as is the situation on the Island, on which everyone conspires to abandon them. They are looked after in a hospice run by the priest, who has just died, and by three old nuns who never leave the building, hence will never come and find them. There is a lighthouse, but the lighthouse-keepers always look out over the sea, so will never notice their predicament. Even the hospice dog refuses to leave his dead master, so will be of no help in guiding them home. The situation is compounded by the danger presented by a hostile nature. They are terrified of the sea, which sounds ever louder, so that they imagine that they are actually within feet of it. The only flowers that grow are asphodels, the 'flowers of the dead'; the rocks and brambles tear their flesh. And we are told that a relentlessly cold winter is about to set in, and the snow we see starting to fall is merely the beginning.

This setting is certainly surreal in one sense—the blind do not live in a world that is related to ordinary life. But while strange, the plight of the waiting blind does not seem meaningless or gratuitous. Instead, we sense a metaphysical dimension to their bewilderment. It would be misleading to attempt to view the play as a definite, clear-cut allegory: symbolist drama like Maeterlinck's derives its power precisely from the fact that the portentous quality is suggestive, not overtly allegorical. These are men and women who have no conception of where they are going in life. They can be seen as lost souls. Their blindness strikes at the very heart of their being—it prevents them not only from seeing each other, but also from feeling for each other, from understanding each other, from loving each other. The dramatic irony of the dead priest's presence in their midst leads the audience to devalue all their capacities, all their conclusions, since they are so patently unfit to judge the situation. Intermittently, they become buoyed up by hope, but we are made to realize that their optimism is futile. And indeed, the play ends on a note of anticlimax, when their belief that rescue is at hand seems to be mistaken—although we cannot be sure even of that.

An additional element is provided by the fact that their guide was a priest. They have in the past relied on a man of religion to help them on their way; but he has involuntarily failed them and doomed them. The strangely threatening island setting seems to contain many of the most daunting features of nature, like a microcosm of a dangerous world: 'there's a mountain no one's climbed, and valleys where people don't like going, and caves that nobody's ever explored.' The sea booms on all sides, the ice cracking beneath the waves. There are marshes to sink into, a huge river to fall into, a dark forest to get lost in. Even the hospice where they feel safe is a grim structure: 'They say it's a very dark and gloomy old castle, no light ever shines there, except in the tower where the priest's room is.' And their safe haven also seems to represent a deplorable lack of initiative—they prefer to hide themselves away behind closed doors in the dormitory, rather than facing the sunlight outside.

On the one hand, these are feeble, puerile, unadventurous people, with an obvious handicap preventing them from seeing the realities of life; but on the other hand, the journey they take is beyond their capacities, and making them go on it has been a cruel deception. It is up to us whether we see the blind as representing mankind, whether the priest is seen as symbolizing religion. There are, after all, twelve blind people, and with the priest that makes thirteen, the same number as Christ and the disciples. Whether or not this is a deliberate parallel, it is undoubtedly true of this play, as of Maeterlinck's others, that there is a sense of a dimension outside the reality of the situation with which we are presented.

On another level, the play has a mystical, faerie quality that was very dear to Maeterlinck. It is embodied in the character of the young blind girl, who is endowed with physical beauty and also with second sight. Whereas the other characters stumble their way across the stage, she unerringly finds her way forward. She can sense which people are going to have unhappy lives in future, and can hear the sound of the stars. The other characters also sense that she is special. The oldest blind man describes the moment when he first became aware of her: 'One night, at prayer time, among the women, I heard a voice I didn't recognize; and I could hear from your voice you were very young... Hearing your voice, I'd have liked to see you as well...' Maeterlinck makes much of her youthful, virginal beauty—she has the same fey quality as his Melisande.

And then who or what is the mysterious presence that the blind sense among them at the end? The audience sees nothing, but the blind are convinced that a woman is coming—they can hear her footsteps and the rustling of her skirts in the dead leaves. And the baby, the only sighted member of the group, looks towards her and wails. Is she death come to claim them?

The setting, too, seems magical, a mysterious Island removed from the rest of the world and seemingly forgotten. The time-scale is vague and indeterminate. Nothing suggests a modern place—the hospice is an ancient castle, any evidence of civilization (dykes, a lighthouse, ships, a church steeple) has existed for hundreds of years. The characters all wear robes. We get no sense of the 1890s here. Even the condition of

blindness and its treatment seem anachronistic. Medical reme-
dies are never mentioned—it is the old priest with his folk-
cures who is, it seems, potentially able to treat the young blind
girl. And none of the characters is clear as to why they are
blind—some of them talk vaguely of having once been able to
see when they were children, but no illness, not even an
awareness of the moment when they went blind, is ever mentioned. There seem to be variations in their blindness—one of
them can see a blue line under his almost-closed eyelids when
there is sunshine, while another says 'My eyelids are closed, but
I can feel my eyes are alive...' These types of blindness are
medically extremely improbable, and the playwright has clearly
not spent time researching the details of the conditions he
describes. The reality and the details of what blindness is really
like are not a central point of interest. The innovative Maeterlinck has rejected realism and instead reverted to an ancient
tradition—to the symbolic blindness of a character from
Shakespeare or Greek tragedy, Gloucester in *King Lear* or
Oedipus Rex.

We are made to concentrate on one particular aspect of
blindness—the helplessness that it induces in sufferers, and
their resulting feelings of anxiety and distress. The characters
in the play, with brief moments of respite, are in a state of
constant near-panic. The play is an almost unrelenting exploration of this state. It cannot be called a tragedy, in that nothing
happens—the one death has occurred before it begins, and at
the end we do not know whether or not the blind will be
rescued. Maeterlinck does little to relieve the atmosphere.
There are episodes of narrative interest, when the characters
describe the priest, narrate their past, or tell what they know of
their island dwelling. There are one or two brief moments of
comic relief—for instance when the blind man who is also deaf

inappropriately starts whining like a street mendicant, where-upon one of the others tells him tartly: 'Be quiet!—This is no time for begging', or the primness with which the priest's supposed departure is greeted: 'People shouldn't go to the seaside at his age!' Most of the twelve characters remain quaint, small-minded, and unimaginative, even though they are over-whelmed by a situation that is beyond their understanding. But while this occasionally makes them seem ridiculous, mostly it merely serves to emphasize the contrast between their own smallness and the enormity of their predicament. Maeterlinck's play is an exploration of the potential for disaster when one thing goes awry. Although the situation seems far-fetched, the fundamental nature of the problem is apparent to everyone. This is what gives the play its power.

Chronologically, *Ubu the King* followed very close after *The Blind*. In character, the two plays are completely different. *Ubu the King* is a mystery. In the first place it is not clear who wrote it. The play, the first of a trilogy (the other two being *Ubu the Cuckold* and *Ubu Bound*), was first published in 1896; at that stage Jarry called it 'A five-act prose drama reconstituted in its entirety, just as it was performed by the puppets of the Théâtre des Phynances in 1888'. In 1888, Jarry was 15, and a schoolboy at the Lycée at Rennes. The Théâtre des Phynances was the name the boys gave to their amateur theatre company. Some years after Jarry's death, a book appeared claiming that the true authors of the play were two schoolfriends of Jarry's, co-founders of the Théâtre des Phynances, Charles and Henri Morin: Jarry's only contribution was the name Ubu. Whatever the extent of Jarry's involvement, it is undoubtedly true that the schoolboy authors were drawing on a wealth of jokes, fantasies, and tall stories woven by generations of pupils round the portly figure of their chemistry teacher, M. Hébert, unable to keep order and terrorized by his teenage charges. Hébert became le Père Heb, Eb, Ebé, and so on, till he reached his final apotheosis as Ubu. It seems we will never know exactly how much of the text is Jarry's: the schoolboys' play was originally written down in a green notebook which has long since disappeared. However, Jarry deserves the credit for seeing the potential of Ubu and bringing him to the attention of the public.

And here we have our second mystery. The play was undoubtedly a scandal when it first appeared, but despite several eyewitness accounts,[1] it is difficult to recapture the true atmosphere of the original production. One contemporary claims that the stage set was designed by a number of distinguished artists and friends of Jarry, notably the painters Bonnard, Vuillard, and Toulouse-Lautrec; another states baldly 'there was no stage set'. Keith Beaumont has sifted through the evidence, and gives a convincing account of what all agree was an evening which shocked the greater part of the largely bourgeois audience.[2] The champions of the play defended it with vigour, the audience came to blows and the auditorium was demolished. The actual performance was halted for some twenty minutes after the first word of the play, 'Merdre!' ('Crrrap!'), which was enough to provoke a complete uproar—and left the audience feeling bewildered and insulted.

But despite its problematic beginnings, there is no doubt about the immediacy and power of the play. *Ubu* hits you

---

[1] See Alfred Jarry, *Ubu*, edited by Noël Arnaud and Henri Bordillon (Gallimard (Folio); Paris, 1978), for extracts from a number of eyewitness accounts.

[2] See Keith Beaumont, *Jarry: Ubu roi* (London: Grant and Cutler, 1987), 59–64. For more details see his *Alfred Jarry: A Critical and Biographical Study* (Leicester University Press, 1984), 99–101.

between the eyes. An outrageous schoolboy joke, it has the impact and directness of a nineteenth-century *Schoolkids' Oz*. It demonstrates a disregard for the conventions that would, I suspect, prove beyond the capacities of any adult writer. There is no concern for consistency of characterization, register, historical background, fantasy, or dialogue. The characters oscillate wildly between intoning grandiose, archaic declamations or fighting duels of honour, and bawling puerile insults—the sort that would raise a groan from a class of teenagers—or braining each other with the abandon of Punch and Judy. Into this crazy mixture the young writers put whatever happened to catch their fancy: technical terms from heraldry (the names of the 'Pillodins' Gyron, Pile, and Cottise are bars on heraldic scutcheons) or sailing (the Captain's orders in Act V are all authentic); allusions to Polish history with its richly named heroes (Stanislas Leczinsky, Jan Sobiesky), echoes of Romantic literature (Queen Rosemonde's name has all the floweriness of the romantic heroine with echoes of the *rosa mundi*, the Virgin Mary). All this jostles with broad lavatorial humour (Ubu gets his guests to suck a filthy lavatory-brush at his banquet), and with surreal farce, as when Ubu bashes his enemies to death with the carcass of a bear, or pops them in his deadly pockets to perish.

So there is little realism in the play. The atmosphere of fantasy must have been enhanced by key features of the first professional production of 1896. Jarry, who was closely involved in the production, insisted that the actors must leave their own personalities at home, and shut themselves inside masks. They were to seem like giant puppets. Even the voices should sound artificial. Jarry observes, oddly: 'the actor must have a special *voice*, which is the voice of the role, as if the hollow mouth of the mask could utter only what the mask would say if its muscles and lips could move.'[3] The stage settings he favoured could have been painted by Magritte: mantelpieces, complete with ornaments and clocks, which split and turn into doors, palm-trees growing at the foot of beds with miniature elephants perched in their fronds. In addition, for practical reasons, he used a different though equally unrealistic technique, introducing scene-changes by means of explanatory placards carried on by a respectably dressed gentleman with a long white beard.

But to Jarry at least the play was much more than pure fantasy. He described it as 'a modern satire', and wished it to appear 'horrific' to the audience. The focus of the satire is, of course, the character of Ubu himself. Ubu, says Jarry, is the audience's double, or rather its 'ignoble double', since he epitomizes base attributes which we all share: gluttony, lewdness, imbecility, and tyranny. Jarry wished Ubu to wear contemporary dress (grey suit, bowler hat) to emphasize the relevance of the satire to modern life. The Polish setting also reinforces the universality of the satire: according to Jarry, Poland was chosen precisely because it did not really exist politically at the time, so it could represent any country: 'as for the action, ... it takes place in Poland, that is to say Nowhere'.

It may, however, be unwise to accept Jarry's comments on his play without demur. He was writing as an adult, some nine years after the play was first performed by the 15-year-old schoolfriends; he was a notoriously eccentric and unreliable witness; and, appropriately enough, his comments on the play, like the play itself, have an iconoclastic quality that calls into question much of what we take for granted.

[3] These remarks come in an article, 'De l'inutilité du théâtre au théâtre' (*Mercure de France*, Sept. 1896). Jarry wrote it to prepare the public for what was to come when *Ubu* was staged.

For if the play has a theme, it is subversion. It undermines the values that Jarry and his fellow 15-year-olds were taught at the lycée. A schoolboy's revenge on the establishment, it mocks at sacred totems such as religion, royalty, courage, filial love, marriage, and the dignity of human life. The play's title is an irreverent allusion to *Oedipus Rex* (as the title of the sequel, *Ubu enchaîné*, is to *Prometheus Bound*). In plot, the play is a crude parody of *Macbeth*: a valued soldier of the king, Ubu is incited by his wife to murder him so as to usurp his crown. A tragic, noble side to the play is sketched in and systematically punctured. King Wenceslas and his family speak in the courtly language and express the elevated sentiments of Corneille or Racine, creating a dignified effect which is intermittently deflated by blatant crudeness. For example, every time the king's youngest son Bougrelas (Buggerlas) is named out loud the dignity of the royal family collapses; and the consistently elevated register of Queen Rosemonde's laments was continually subverted in the original production by the fact that she spoke with a strong Cantal accent (the French equivalent of Mummerset). A similar technique undermines every detail of character presentation and plot. On the one hand King Wenceslas nobly trusts Ubu, and goes unarmed to the parade where he is to meet his tragic death. On the other, his inspection techniques at parades can scarcely be taken seriously: he wears iron shoes to kick people with if they don't meet with his approval. And even the manner of the king's betrayal and assassination are uproarious: Ubu gives the signal for the conspirators to attack by stamping on his foot and shouting 'Merdre!' ('Crrrap!').

The play excels by virtue of the extraordinary gusto with which it demolishes its targets. The text is, in fact, painstakingly composed, with every detail lovingly dwelt on. It has exactly the same feel to it as the elaborate obscene poems that clever schoolchildren recite together, naughtily and in secret, lurking in corners of the playground. Lavish details are heaped up, many of which are jokes. In the original edition, the instruments supposed to be playing in the theatre orchestra were listed, some of them real, others ridiculous (a sausage figured among the bassoons and big bass drums). In the actual performance, there was a simple piano. When Ubu invites his fellow-conspirators to dinner, the dishes on the menu combine puns and jokes, luscious coinages, extravagant fantasy, and scatological humour.

The characters also exemplify the two qualities of subversion and energy. Ubu has something of the traditional *matamore* of French comedy, the braggart soldier whose arrogance and boastfulness are matched only by his cowardice the moment he is threatened. He also reminds one irresistibly of Falstaff. But even this already comic stereotype is further undermined by Jarry, who makes him fluctuate wildly between snivelling with fear and vicious bullying. In addition, Ubu is outrageously babyish; he blubs for his bottle, and in spite of his obscene expletives seems oddly innocent sexually (this is another difference from the braggart soldier, who is forward and flirtatious with women). Ubu's pleasures are oral and anal, his fears those of a tiny child. Like a baby, too, he is conscienceless. The suffering of the crowds of victims whom he consigns to the trapdoor or to his murderous pockets leaves him completely unmoved. His cruelty would be chilling if it were not so excessive. As his confederate Captain Brubbish tells him, 'In the five days that you've been king, you've committed more murders than would be needed to damn all the saints in Paradise to perdition'. Overall, this is a character who is simply not governed by human instincts. The audience may find it difficult to respond to Ubu's actions: mostly, his excesses are funny, but sometimes the chilling implications do strike home, and interfere with the laughter.

Despite his obscenity and his babyishness, Ubu does not seem like a child in one respect: he is too pompous and too hectoring. He is portrayed as a middle-aged man seen through youthful eyes. The very name 'Père Ubu' implies that he is being viewed from the perspective of people young enough to be his children—in French, calling someone 'Père' is an irreverent way of implying that one regards him as old. The fact that Ubu was originally modelled on Jarry's chemistry teacher, Hébert ('who represented... everything that is most grotesque in the world', wrote Jarry), still lurks behind the character. The baby-talk and puerile obscenity mask a hectoring, didactic tone reminiscent of the schoolteacher.

One problem with the characterization is inconsistency. Jarry delights in making the characters behave 'out of character'. Mère Ubu seems firmly drawn in as a prosaic woman, whose ambition is as unimaginative as her food is disgusting. But suddenly she appears as a vamp, two-timing her husband and describing herself as a Venus. Again, Buggerlas sometimes seems like a hilarious exaggeration of the noble young prince, but at other times strikes a pathetic note—and an additional incongruity was provided by his costume in the 1896 production, when he was dressed as an outsize baby, in skirts and a bonnet. Captain Brubbish cheerfully murders his king, then becomes a loyal nobleman. And so on. Ubu himself, of course, changes bewilderingly, from coward to bully, from wailing brat to death-dealing monster, from hero of melodrama to fall-guy of farce, though continuity is maintained by his oaths ('crrrap!' and 'by the wick of my candle!'), or by the phallic accessories that hang from his person in increasing numbers as the play progresses.[4]

As for the language, it shifts in register to encompass the range of subjects that Jarry subverts, incorporating the rhythms and vocabulary of classical tragedy, baby-talk, and obscenity; it reflects the gusto and energy of the plot, for instance in the vitality and variety of the expletives; it teems with technical terms relating to the subjects that have caught the fancy of the author; it sparkles with youthful imagination. Coinages abound; sounds are rolled round the tongue. In particular, Ubu frequently uses the syllable 'bou' or simply 'ou', a fat, lumbering sound that portrays the spherical shape Jarry said represented Ubu himself. Jarry uses it inventively throughout the text. Important, memorable words are 'bouffre', 'bouteille', and many of his coinages: 'gidouille', 'bouzine', or 'boudouille', and the name of 'Bougrelas'. Ubu's speeches also use fruity *r*s, which the actor should pronounce with exaggerated emphasis, starting with the first word of the play, 'Merdre!' Overall, the sound of Ubu's words in the original has weight to it: if you speak them out loud you *have* to declaim them.

For a reader gripped by the character and doings of Ubu, *Ubu the King* is only the beginning. The Ubu material that Jarry has left us also includes poems, pictures, stories, fragments, and even almanacs, and runs to many hundreds of pages. This play is the most accomplished manifestation of what clearly became an obsession with Jarry. His voice and his whole bearing changed—one of his early friends, the poet Léon-Paul Fargue, commented that his manner of speech as a very young man was different before he became completely dominated by Ubu: 'He

---

[4] The original costumes had Ubu ending up in III. 8 with 'at his belt a sabre, a hook, scissors, a knife, his usual cane in his right-hand pocket. A bottle bumping against his rump' (reproduced in *Tout Ubu*).

spoke rapidly, in a clear, pleasant voice which as yet had nothing of that artificial harshness, of that Ubuesque accent, of those attitudes which he was to adopt subsequently.'[5] Jarry became a victim as well as creator of the horrific Père Ubu, unable to shake off the notoriety and power of his own monstrous brain-child. Small wonder that he took refuge in alcohol. When he died, at only 34, Apollinaire described attending his funeral as 'following the hearse of Père Ubu'. He adds: 'We were singing, drinking, and eating cold sausage: a picture of eccentricity like a description invented by the man we were consigning to the earth.' Ubu may have shackled his creator, but he had, and still has, a liberating impact on others.

The third play in this edition, *The Mammaries of Tiresias*, marks the true beginning of surrealism. But curiously, since the genre seems to imply a completely new, abstract way of looking at the world, it reflects its author's life and tastes more directly than the other two works do theirs. Indeed, it is impossible to grasp its essence without knowing something about Apollinaire.

Born in Rome in 1880, he was the illegitimate son of a Polish girl, of wild habits and ancient lineage, Angelica de Kostrowitzky. His real name was Wilhelm de Kostrowitzky; he chose as his *nom de plume* a French version of his middle name, Apollinaris. His father is generally believed to have been an Italian army officer, Francesco Flugi d'Aspremont, though Apollinaire himself encouraged the belief that he had been sired by the son of Napoleon I, L'Aiglon, who did indeed befriend his unconventional mother. Small wonder then that Therese, his anti-heroine, is a fierce, independent woman with small regard for convention. She is viewed throughout the play

---

[5] Quoted in Beaumont, *Alfred Jarry*, 32.

as omnipotent, announcing proudly 'And now the universe will be mine | Women will be mine the government will be mine', but at the same time she has violent, murderous instincts. Above all, she regards motherhood with strong feelings of antagonism. The poor, dutiful husband is left not only to bring up the children, but even to give birth to them—but in the end, with exemplary forbearance, forgives Therese and takes her back.

An even more important element in Apollinaire's life, which is reflected in his play, was his central role in the cultural and artistic life of Paris at the time. He was fascinated by everything new or avant-garde. The latest intellectual and literary trends, many of which he had a hand in creating, are reflected in all his writing, including *Tiresias*. Like other forward-looking writers and artists, he systematically exploits the modern world. His setting is not like Maeterlinck's, resolutely excluding modernity. On the contrary, Apollinaire wittily incorporates references to modern communications, in the spoof telegrams which announce absurd new trends in the arts, or in the comic references to newspapers and the telephone. There is even a mention of electricity, which is supposed to illuminate Therese's head-dress when she enters disguised as a fortune-teller. More seriously, Apollinaire begins his play with a long introduction spoken by the director of the troupe, a thinly disguised authorial mouthpiece, who speaks movingly of his experiences in the trenches during the First World War, and also discusses modern trends in the theatre and new ways of staging plays:

> A theatre in the round with two stages
> One in the middle the other like a ring
> Round the audience that would give us scope
> To display our modern art to the full

Jarry's determination to undermine all conventions of staging, so that they had to be rethought, has clearly borne fruit with Apollinaire, who has re-evaluated what, for a nineteenth-century audience, constituted a 'proper' theatre: proscenium arch, illuminated stage, curtain that rises, audience facing the front.

Apollinaire's fascination with the modern world is particularly telling when it comes to the arts. As a young journalist, he rapidly became famous as an art critic, and was the first to introduce to the public the flower of the creative artists of the time. The painters Picasso, Braque, and Matisse, mentioned in *Tiresias*, were his friends, as were many others such as Delaunay, Vlaminck, and Rousseau. And the most important of his many unhappy love-affairs was with the painter Marie Laurencin, with whom he lived for five stormy years, and for whom he wrote some of his most beautiful lyrical love poetry.

The artistic sensibility that was so important to Apollinaire in his life is mirrored in his play, in the vivid, imaginative costumes he invents for the characters (Therese has a '*Blue face, long blue dress decorated with painted monkeys and fruit*'), or in the landscape of Zanzibar, reflected in the lines spoken by the characters, which reminds one of an exotic painting by Rousseau or Gauguin, with its strawberry groves, its banana trees, its elephants and monkeys.

One of the attributes of modern painting which most attracted Apollinaire was the sheer intensity of the effects, the use of vivid colour and the juxtaposition of unexpected objects (one thinks of the floating Eiffel Tower in Delaunay's famous painting, or the newspaper cuttings shaped into musical instruments in the cubist paintings of Picasso or Braque). Apollinaire's writing has been described as the literary equivalent of this collage technique—and this is where we approach surrealism as we know it today. In the Director's opening speech,

Apollinaire describes his conscious desire to produce exciting juxtapositions in his play:

> As in life often linking unrelated
> Sounds gestures colours shouts noise
> Music dance acrobatics poetry painting
> Choruses actions and multiple sets

In the play, extraordinary events and juxtapositions are presented without comment—a woman suddenly grows a moustache, we are shown a chamber-pot and told it is a piano, and treated to mystifying throwaway remarks like 'It's as simple as a periscope'. In the hands of Apollinaire, this technique seems lively and witty. It is, I think, quite surprising to discover from the Preface how serious his ulterior purpose is, when he is so tongue-in-cheek within the play proper—unless the Preface was a belated attempt to make this irreverent farce seem nationalistic. Like *Ubu*, *Tiresias* seems to suggest distrust of serious or moving subjects. Deaths mean nothing—the characters just get back up again after being shot with cardboard Brownings. Greek myth is subverted and mocked when the blind seer Tiresias is portrayed as a bearded lady with balloons for breasts. Love, marriage, and parenthood are laughed at in a variety of different ways—in the ardent wooing of the husband by the policeman, in the reversal of roles between Therese and her husband, in the way the husband brings up his 40,049 infants, alternately extolling the joys of parenthood and shouting at the brats to shut up. This comic surrealism is one of the most attractive qualities of the play—Apollinaire's vivid imagination is working overtime.

The other fascinating and original quality of the play is undoubtedly its style. Apollinaire is, after all, best known for his poetry, and this play is very much the work of a poet. In this, he writes very differently from both Maeterlinck and Jarry. Maeterlinck's style is limpid in its simplicity. Jarry's is parodic and crude. But linguistically Apollinaire's play is sophisticated and self-aware. He varies the register constantly. Often he breaks into rhyme. The text is full of puns and word-plays. He uses refrains and choruses as though he were writing music—this one recurs several times:

> HEY! SHEPHERDESS COME SMOKE YOUR PIPE
> AND I WILL PLAY MY PIPES FOR YOU
> YET IN SEVEN YEARS THE BAKER'S WIFE
> WILL SHED HER SKIN FOR ONE THAT'S NEW
> EVERY SEVEN YEARS WHAT A LIFE

He varies his language from the colloquial to the recondite, from the modern to the old-fashioned. A portentous statement such as this:

> People have too good an opinion
> Of humanity and its leavings
> Does the excrement of jewellers
> Contain pearls and diamonds

jostles with inelegant, casual remarks like: 'It stinks of crime round here.' And there is a wealth of imagery. For example, Therese exclaims: 'I look like a cornfield ready for the combine harvester', and the journalist child tells his father:

> The printing presses are like trees
> Leaf upon leaf flaps in the breeze
> The papers have grown they're ready to pick
> To make a salad to feed the kids . . .

There are figures of speech and verbal pyrotechnics of all kinds to remind us that the author is an accredited poet. This may be one of the reasons that the play is most frequently performed in

Poulenc's sung version—the language is so lyrical that it reads like a libretto.[6]

One curious innovation that Apollinaire brought to his poetry, including this play, is to dispense altogether with punctuation. From the poetic point of view, this creates a suggestive, uncertain atmosphere. It is sometimes unclear whether a word refers back to what precedes it, or forward to what follows it. A clear example is the first verse of the poem 'Sous le Pont Mirabeau', a love poem written when his relationship with Marie Laurencin had failed:

> Sous le pont Mirabeau coule la Seine
> > Et nos amours
> > Faut-il qu'il m'en souvienne
> > La joie venait toujours après la peine

> *Beneath the Pont Mirabeau flows the Seine*
> > *And our love*
> > *Must I remember*
> > *Joy always followed suffering*

The second line could refer back to the first—our love is flowing away just as the water is flowing away. Or it could link forward to the next line—must I keep remembering our love? The same ambiguity haunts the third line. The result is more evocative than a 'correctly' punctuated verse could ever be. The same mysterious quality pervades the written text of *Tiresias*. It is up to the actor to reproduce this ambiguity in his performance.

Tiresias, with its introductory manifesto, its emphasis on linguistic niceties, and its imaginative stage directions, is as interesting to read as to see. As a performance text, however, it

---

[6] The libretto of Poulenc's opera, which has the same name as the play, incorporates most of the text.

achieved immediate notoriety, and the first and only performance during Apollinaire's lifetime enjoyed a *succès de scandale*. It continues to be regarded as a landmark in theatre, though rarely performed. Today's actors, trained to render the complexity and ambiguity of modern works by such as Beckett, Albee, or Pinter, would be excellently placed to do it justice. The time is ripe for a major revival.

Maeterlinck, Jarry, and Apollinaire were all vital in shaping the theatre of the twentieth century; but in the earlier years of the century Maeterlinck was undoubtedly the best known. It was not just that he was an establishment figure, acknowledged as one of the greatest francophone writers of his age (he was awarded the Nobel Prize in 1911). But his influence extended far outside the French-speaking world. He was seen as an innovator, bringing a modern, abstract quality to the theatre. He was particularly admired in Russia, and Chekhov used him as a source of inspiration. The avant-garde play within a play written by Treplev in *The Seagull*, with its apocalyptic vision of a dying world, is a pastiche of Maeterlinck; but it is not a disrespectful one. Maeterlinck's vision was of man no longer set in an ordinary world, but locked in deadly conflict with the cataclysmic power of the elements. The eagerness with which the Russians accepted this world-view is summed up by the poet Alexander Blok: 'The sun of naïve realism has set; it is impossible to give a meaning to anything at all outside symbolism.'[7] More recently, a joint Russian–American film of Maeterlinck's *The Blue Bird* was made, featuring Elizabeth Taylor.

English-speaking playwrights were equally inspired by Maeterlinck. The plays of W. B. Yeats are obvious cases in point.

[7] Essay 'On the Present State of Russian Symbolism', quoted in T. G. West (ed.), *Symbolism: An Anthology* (London: Methuen, 1980), 152.

Yeats adopts the mystical quality, the links with ancient legend, the more portentous and poetical side of Maeterlinck the symbolist playwright. Yeats sees Maeterlinck as a sort of high priest of theatre, 'a foreshadower of the new sacred book, of which all the arts ... are beginning to dream'.[8] This emphasis on the 'sacred' nature of theatre was to continue after Yeats—its influence can be readily detected in the plays of T. S. Eliot or Christopher Fry; and as recently as 1968 the director Peter Brook divided modern theatre into Holy Theatre and Rough Theatre.[9] Maeterlinck is without a doubt the pioneer of Holy Theatre.

In the French-speaking world, Maeterlinck was regarded as modern, innovative, and daring. Proust mentions him several times as the quintessence of the avant-garde, and stresses his strange modern ideas and his determined rejection of realism. One of the most daring of his plays was *The Seven Princesses* (written just after *The Blind* in 1891). This play broke new ground in that it made an important feature of silence, again discarding both the emphasis on words of French classical theatre and the naturalism of Zola. Instead, it reverted to ancient tradition (Greek tragedies had silent actors who communicated through mime, and Shakespeare had mute figures like the touching Lavinia in *Titus Andronicus*). Maeterlinck's seven princesses did not speak because they were asleep. This emphasis on silence is already apparent in *The Blind*, with the character of the dead priest, who occupies the centre stage, and is clearly meant to be the first person to capture the audience's attention, as we can tell from the stage directions. And yet he neither speaks nor moves throughout the play. The idea of a

---

[8] Essay 'The Symbolism of Poetry', quoted in West, *Symbolism*, 21.
[9] *The Empty Space*, (London: Macgibbon and Kee, 1968).

theatre of silence is familiar to modern audiences from famous characters like the mute girl Kattrin in Brecht's *Mother Courage*. Maeterlinck controls his use of silence—he dramatizes it without taking it to its logical conclusion. It was to reach its apotheosis—and a dead end—with Beckett's *Breath*, in which the curtain goes up on a stage empty of characters, and no words are spoken. In the 1890s the concept must have seemed shockingly innovative.

Maeterlinck outlived his own notoriety, and came to be viewed very much as an establishment figure. With the single exception of *Pelleas and Melisande*, his work is rarely performed in English nowadays, though *The Blind* continues to be popular with Belgian directors. But echoes of his ideas abound in modern French, English, and American theatre.[10] Perhaps the most unexpected parallel is with the theatre of Samuel Beckett, whose most famous play, *Waiting for Godot*, is remarkably similar to *The Blind*. The story in both cases is of a long wait, by characters whose personalities are ordinary and trivial, but whose origins are mysterious. A nameless threat seems to menace them—or perhaps it doesn't really. There is even the presence of blindness in both plays, since Beckett's Pozzo is mysteriously struck blind from one act to the next. Other Beckett plays also remind one of *The Blind*, notably *Happy Days*, with Minnie's motionless presence centre stage throughout, like that of the dead priest. Beckett has discarded the portentous, mystical side of Maeterlinck's play, but retained its daring simplicity and above all its powerfully enigmatic quality. These aspects of Maeterlinck have survived into the avant-garde and the Theatre of the Absurd.

---

[10] Katharine Worth, *Maeterlinck's Plays in Performance* (Cambridge: Chadwyck–Healey, 1985) draws attention to the parallels with Pinter and Albee as well as with Beckett.

It is perhaps surprising that Jarry greatly admired Maeterlinck, since the Belgian writer is almost classically limpid, while the iconoclastic Frenchman makes a feature of lack of discipline. Nevertheless, amongst some notes found after Jarry's death, there is the following unsolicited tribute:

Among us is a tragic author, possessing new terrors and pities, so private that it is pointless for him to express them in any other way but silence: Maurice Maeterlinck. We are convinced that we are witnessing a rebirth of theatre, for in France for the first time there is an ABSTRACT theatre, and at last we can read, without the trouble of a translation, plays as eternally tragic as those by Ben Jonson, Marlowe, Shakespeare, Cyril Tourneur, Goethe.[11]

Unlike *The Blind*, Jarry's *Ubu the King* is still performed, and in prestigious productions, like that of Peter Brook in 1977. Although Jarry wrote copiously throughout his short life, his reputation rests almost entirely on this play, undoubtedly his masterpiece. Its influence was both immediate and lasting. Most obviously, we see it in the powerful mixture of cruelty and comedy which Jarry inherited from traditional knockabout farce, but took to ludicrous extremes. Audiences today are still simultaneously shocked and thrilled by this combination, which is one reason for the popularity of films by Tarantino, Scorsese, or John Walters. Peter Brook's division of modern theatre into Holy Theatre and Rough Theatre applies as much to Jarry as to Maeterlinck. Jarry's play, with its loose ends, its obscenities, its brutality, its puerility, is probably the most perfect example of Rough Theatre that exists.

Jarry was a fine classical scholar, well acquainted with Ancient Greek drama. In his hands, the pared-down quality

---

[11] Jarry was responding to a questionnaire on dramatic art, but these pages were not published till after his death. See *Œuvres complètes*, i. 411.

of Greek theatre, with its masked characters and choruses, turns into an extravaganza which goes far beyond the bounds of plausibility. Jarry made a point of stressing the artificiality of his play. For instance, in the production notes, he describes the result he aims for in the crowd scenes as follows: 'Doing away with crowds, which are often clumsy on stage and impede understanding. Therefore, a single soldier in the review scene, a single soldier in the jostle and scramble in which Ubu says: "What a mob!" '[12] The National Theatre of Brent, a two-man act specializing in ludicrous versions of major plays, has recently adopted the same technique to considerable comic effect.

Many of Jarry's ideas for making his play seem more fabricated and artificial are copied to this day: the adoption of special stage voices, the conscious re-creation of a Punch and Judy effect, the rejection of a detailed set in favour of a plain background, the abandonment of set changes, the discarding of the curtain. Jarry's techniques still make a production seem modern even a hundred years later—for instance he plumped for 'costumes as lacking in local colour or historical accuracy as possible'—an idea congenial to many a present-day director. At times, like Maeterlinck, Jarry discards the trends of nineteenth-century theatre in favour of tradition. Jarry's instruction that 'The actors must always be aware of the audience' represents such a reversal, rejecting the more recent suspension of disbelief characteristic both of naturalism and of nineteenth-century romanticism. As was the custom in traditional theatre from tragedy to pantomime, he makes his actors connive with the audience.

[12] Jarry wrote these notes about how he wanted his play performed to Lugné-Poe; see *Tout Ubu*, 133.

Jarry's systematic abandonment of all the conventions of nineteenth-century theatre was the act of a genuine lateral thinker and eccentric. It is this undoubted originality which means that he continues to retain his place as a pioneer, and that his work seems new and different to succeeding generations. His revolutionary approach has been copied by playwrights and directors, for instance Antonin Artaud and Roger Vitrac, who in 1927 founded the Théâtre Alfred Jarry, with the express aim of achieving 'the ruin of the theatre as it exists today in France'.

Jarry's influence extended beyond the theatre to the realms of thought. He invented a spoof school of philosophy called 'Pataphysics'. Roger Shattuck describes the process as follows: 'He set about to upset the balance of waking (rational) logic and developed the elements of 'Pataphysicks, a kind of reasonable unreason similar to the workings of our dreaming minds.'[13] The same Jarry who turned theatrical convention on its head was at work, inventing a cult of anti-reason. Pataphysics became a major literary movement when it was revived in 1949 with the founding of the Collège de Pataphysique. This had strong affinities with another school founded in 1960, OuLiPo, much inspired by the Pataphysicians' pursuit of pointless and complicated intellectual mind-benders. The leading light was the anarchic poet, novelist, and philosopher Raymond Queneau; members included the Italian Italo Calvino, the American Harry Matthews, and the Frenchman Georges Perec. Perec's great novel *Life: A User's Manual* (1978) reflects Jarry's ludic lateral-thinking approach. So Jarry has made his mark not only on the theatre but on the novel, not only on his own time but on the present day.

[13] *The Banquet Years* (London: Jonathan Cape, 1969), 157.

Closer to his own time, Jarry had enormous influence on the surrealist movement. Apollinaire was his friend and admirer, and his play picks up many of the traits that we find in *Ubu*. Apollinaire also rejects realism in theatre. Photographs of the only contemporary production of *The Mammaries of Tiresias* reveal cubist costumes and artificial make-up. The stage directions also show a deliberate search for artifice: speeches are to be delivered through a megaphone, dead bodies to come to life, and so on.

But undoubtedly the most influential aspect of Apollinaire's play was the playwright's invention of the term 'surrealism' to describe it. No sooner had *Tiresias* become public property than a new generation of writers adopted surrealism as their *raison d'être*. It was at the première of *Tiresias* that André Breton, later one of the greatest exponents of surrealism, met the poet Paul Éluard. The surrealists built on the quirky, witty shock-effects that Apollinaire had presented deadpan to an outraged public: a woman with detachable breasts and a beard, a man who gives birth, a chamber-pot which is called a piano. The aim of the surrealists was to shock by juxtaposing objects that were not normally put together. Items like Meret Oppenheim's fur-lined teacup and saucer or Man Ray's sky-blue French loaf are obvious examples. Presenting these objects invites the public to view them in a new light, and liberates us from our dull, conventional attitudes. The importance of this movement in theatre, literature, and the visual arts cannot be too strongly stressed. We have all been exposed to the concept of surrealism and conditioned to respond to it—and advertisers trade on this fact, knowing that we will react positively to cigarette packets being presented as gold ingots or Egyptian pyramids.

This has become the benign face of surrealism; but it had its more brutal side too. It was at the première of *Tiresias* that

Vaché threatened the audience with a gun,[14] demonstrating a more radical response to Apollinaire's work, later to be crystallized into the Dada movement, an angry, anti-establishment variety of surrealism. Dada responded to the anarchic qualities of both Jarry and Apollinaire by taking them to extremes. Apollinaire's play had ridiculed authority in a number of ways, for example presenting the police, the government, and the press as corrupt (a policeman makes a pass at a member of the public, a member of parliament keeps mistresses, a journalist invents the news). Dada takes this trend much further, systematically rejecting all authority. The most important difference is that Apollinaire had a serious reforming purpose, whereas Dada practised anarchy and violence for their own sakes.

In French theatre, film, literature, and criticism the surrealist movement proper was followed by a succession of different schools; but these have tended to incorporate Maeterlinck's sense of metaphysical anguish, and Apollinaire's and Jarry's lateral-thinking rejection of the status quo. To give a few examples, the Theatre of the Absurd, as represented by playwrights like Ionesco or Beckett, cultivated both a sense of unfocused distress reminiscent of *The Blind*, and a richly comic vein of meaninglessness and nonsense. Avant-garde film directors like Cocteau, and later Jean-Luc Godard, sought for what was new and arresting in all respects—in the lack of plot, the unexpected juxtapositions, and the off-beat responses of the characters. With the *nouveau roman*, novelists like Alain Robbe-Grillet rejected traditional plot, characterization, and meaningful description, but preserved a sense of menace.

---

[14] Jacques Vaché (1895–1919), dandy, anarchist, and poet (though he didn't write a single line of poetry).

Even the critics felt the need to reject convention and force the public to view the works they were analysing in a new light: for instance with Deconstruction, which aimed to destroy the conventional approach to a text and to make us read it in a new way. It is in this climate that modern French culture is evolving today, and the creators of the present owe an immense debt to these three pioneering playwrights.

NOTE ON THE TRANSLATION

IN translating these three plays, my aim has been fidelity to the original. But they present three very distinct challenges.

The Blind is written in pared-down, simple, but also timeless language. I aimed for a classical, unobtrusive idiom: the audience must be able to imagine the words being spoken by mysterious blind outcasts on an island outside time. Accordingly, I have tried to avoid modern slang; but old-fashioned, dignified words are also inappropriate. This is a text in which the language should not attract attention for its own sake.

With *Ubu the King*, the case is very different. The language is supremely self-conscious and bewilderingly diverse. It seemed vital to vary the registers of the speech, and not to underplay the difference between the exaggeratedly elevated discourse and the crude vulgarity that punctures the effect. The result is to diminish the naturalness of the lines—but if the play sounds natural it ceases to seem extraordinary. Another striking feature is the play's energy. Rendering this requires an uninhibited translator. It seemed to me that this would involve something much more subtle than a free and easy smattering of four-letter words. A permanently racy, slangy style simply fails to echo the original. Some of the liveliest language seems so because it is so contrived—colloquialisms jostle with weird bombast, registers clash. Take Ubu's audience with King Wenceslas:

Père UBU

And now, I must piss off. (*As he turns away, he falls*) Ouch! Ow! Help! By the wick of my candle, I've exploded my intestines and punctured my paunch!

THE KING,
raising him up

Père Ubu, are you hurt?

Père UBU

Yea, verily, and I must surely kick the bucket.

The individual words too can be eccentric and extravagant: the play is remarkable for its wealth of pungent oaths, many of which have an irreligious, old-world and Rabelaisian feel to them. These are particularly difficult to translate—English cannot match French for expletives. Ubu's oaths give the play much of its character, and their effect can be complex. 'Merdre!', the first word in the play, the word which sets the tone of the whole, is immediately recognizable as an enriched form of *merde*. The impact is partly due to the dense juxtaposition of consonants *rdr*.

Ubu often appears archaic: despite Jarry's disingenuous claim that it owed nothing to Rabelais or Shakespeare and was more like Musset, the play is unashamedly stuffed with echoes of these and other earlier writers. Because of links with French tragedy, as well as the parallels with *Macbeth*, I decided to include a few recognizable phrases from Shakespeare's play, as the most consistent inspiration.

More subtle are the echoes of rhythms from other types of work. For example, when Mère Ubu is hunting for the treasure in the crypt (IV. i), she breaks into alexandrines, the twelve-syllable lines that are used in French classical tragedy, and which therefore imply the noblest and most serious of registers. These lines are surreptitiously tucked into her prose, and might be overlooked by a reader; but the actress should bring them out in her performance. The nearest English equivalent is the iambic pentameter, with its Shakespearean atmosphere. Accordingly, I include some in my translation.

Most difficult of all are the constant punning, double meanings, and word-plays. You have only to look at the characters' names to see how complicated they can be to translate: take the case of le capitaine Bordure, who becomes Captain Brubbish in my version. The original name is derived from the same heraldic source as the three Pillodins Gyron, Pile, and Cottise: the *bordure* is the border round a scutcheon. But the name also suggests rubbish (*b-ordure*). It was not possible to incorporate both allusions in the translation, because in English 'ordure' is not the normal, everyday word for rubbish as it is in French. Brubbish's name must undermine his image as a decent, honourable soldier every time it is pronounced. In the original production, as it happens, the character seemed yet more farcical, as he was made to speak with an exaggerated English accent, a parody of a *milor'*.

The Mammaries of Tiresias is also linguistically self-aware, but in a very different way. The Director's Prologue adopts a serious, heartfelt tone. But in the rest of the play, the most frequent register is light-hearted, an off-beat wit that belies and perhaps undermines its serious purpose. It seems that Apollinaire cannot resist the temptation to pun, joke, burst into rhyme, transforming his text into a sustained exercise in humour. The translator's first problem with this idiosyncratic, poetic text is Apollinaire's absence of punctuation, which, as I have suggested in the Introduction, creates an atmosphere of mystery and ambiguity. The potential nuances must be noted and reproduced as far as possible. Then there is the poet's sense of rhythm and fondness for rhyme. Blank verse and rhyming verse are constantly interpolated into more mundane text. I have reproduced this effect where it occurs. Although translators sometimes argue that rhyming plays seem more artificial in English than in French, I do not believe this to be the case with this play. The original French text is unashamedly artificial: colloquialisms jostle with alexandrines, rhyming choruses recur as in a song, and many different registers of speech are juxtaposed, to create a patchwork effect that is more colourful than realistic. The Husband varies from talking in simple colloquialisms: ('Are you the barber short back and sides please') to dignified, portentous utterances ('Great representative of high authority | You hear what has been said I feel with clarity'), or obscenities ('Parisiennes are nice | Much nicer than the rest | If pussies all love mice | We love your pussies best'). He uses rhyme, as in the last example; official-sounding jargon ('Excuse me Monsieur if you have business with me | Be so good as to take | My military papers out of my left-hand pocket'); and lyrical, romantic outpourings which he then proceeds to undermine. In addition, the text offers spoof newspaper headlines, telegrams, official documents, and many other types of language.

The translator's worst problem is, of course, punning and word-play. Apollinaire is fond of puns, sometimes rather heavily contrived ones. The most laboured example is the indignant husband's verdict on his errant wife:

THE HUSBAND

My wife's a man-madame
She's gone off with the piano the violin the butter-dish
She's a soldier a minister a phy-shit-ian

THE POLICEMAN

Phy-tits-ian

xlvi

THE HUSBAND

She's exploded *them* so she's more of a phy-shit-ian

Apollinaire revels in such elaborate verbal jokes. There is an innocence about his writing, an unashamed enjoyment of making artificial patterns out of language, that seems endearingly childlike.

An important point of comparison between the three playwrights is their respective awareness of their plays as performance texts. Although he was at the start of his career, Maeterlinck was already an acknowledged playwright when he wrote *The Blind*: his work was intended for performance, and comes over seamlessly when read aloud. Jarry was determinedly eccentric, but it is nevertheless clear that *Ubu the King* was also written for performance. After all, the earliest drafts were performed when he was still a schoolboy. And his desperate eagerness to have the play staged indicates that he intended it above all for performance. The same is not true of Apollinaire. He claimed that *Tiresias* was written years before he was finally asked to offer it to a director. Whether or not this is true is a moot point; but the fact remains that he did not see fit to stress the performance aspect—he promoted his play as a gratuitous exercise in creativity, and maintained that he was happy to leave it for years without any thought of performance. It was almost in spite of himself that he created a work that comes across vividly on stage. This fact makes Apollinaire's text particularly challenging to translate. But then, as I have said, all three plays have provided their own individual challenges.

M.S.

SELECT BIBLIOGRAPHY

MAURICE MAETERLINCK

Theatre

Most of Maeterlinck's plays were translated when they first appeared.
See:

The Plays of Maurice Maeterlinck, 2 vols., trans. R. Hovey (Chicago and New York: Herbert Stone, 1905).

The Blue Bird, trans. Alexander Teixeira de Mateos (London: Methuen, 1909).

The Treasure of the Humble, trans. A. Sutro (London: G. Allen, 1897). Contains an interesting essay on theatre.

Maeterlinck's early plays in French, including *Les Aveugles*, are available in a convenient modern edition:

Maurice Maeterlinck, *Théâtre*, ed. M. de Rougemont (Geneva: Slatkine, 1979).

Biography and Criticism

CLARK, MACDONALD, *Maurice Maeterlinck, Poet and Philosopher* (New York: Frederick Stokes, 1916). Useful analysis of Maeterlinck's philosophical ideas in the early part of his career.

HALLS, W. D., *Maurice Maeterlinck: A Study of his Life and Thought* (Oxford: Clarendon Press, 1960). A lively, detailed biography. Full bibliography.

KNAPP, BETTINA, *Maurice Maeterlinck* (Boston: Twayne, 1975). An excellent chronological critical study with biographical details. Useful bibliography.

KONRAD, LINN B., 'Symbolic Action in Modern Drama: Maurice Maeterlinck', in James Redmond (ed.), *Themes in Drama*, 4, (Cambridge University Press, 1982). On Maeterlinck and symbolism.

WORTH, KATHARINE J., *Maeterlinck's Plays in Performance* (Theatre in Focus; Cambridge: Chadwyck–Healey, 1985). Slides of original and modern productions with accompanying text. Interesting and informative.

JARRY AND APOLLINAIRE

SCHUMACHER, CLAUDE, *Alfred Jarry and Guillaume Apollinaire*, (Macmillan Modern Dramatists; London: Macmillan, 1984). Lively introduction to the two writers and their background. Focuses on Apollinaire's theatre (overlooked by most critics).

SHATTUCK, ROGER, *The Banquet Years* (London: Jonathan Cape, 1969). Excellent study of the cultural scene in the Paris of the time, with detailed accounts of Jarry and Apollinaire.

ALFRED JARRY

Works in English

Caesar Antichrist, trans. Antony Melville (London: Atlas Press, 1992).

Selected Works, ed. Roger Shattuck and Simon Watson Taylor (London: Methuen, 1965).

The Supermale: A Modern Novel, trans. Barbara Wright (London: Jonathan Cape, 1968).

The following editions in French are recommended:

Tout Ubu, ed. Maurice Saillet (Paris: Livre de Poche, 1962).

Œuvres complètes, i, ed. Michel Arrivé (Paris: Gallimard (Pléiade), 1972).

Biography and Criticism

BEAUMONT, KEITH, *Alfred Jarry: A Critical and Biographical Study* (Leicester University Press, 1984). The fullest account of the life and works. Scholarly and readable.

—— *Jarry: Ubu roi* (Critical Guides to French Texts, 69; London: Grant and Cutler, 1987). An excellent pithy account.

Select Bibliography

ESSLIN, MARTIN, *The Theatre of the Absurd* (Harmondsworth: Penguin, 1961).

LABELLE, MAURICE MARC, *Alfred Jarry, Nihilism and the Theater of the Absurd* (New York University Press, 1980).

GUILLAUME APOLLINAIRE

Works in English

Apollinaire on Art: Essays and Reviews, 1902–1918, ed. LeRoy C. Breunig and Susan Suleiman (New York: Viking Press, 1972).

Calligrammes: Poems of Peace and War, 1913–1916, trans. Anne Hyde Greet (Berkeley and Los Angeles: University of California Press), 1980.

The Cubist Painters: Aesthetic Meditations, 1913, trans. Lionel Abel (New York: Wittenborn, 1962).

The Heresiarch and Co., trans. Remy Inglis Hall (New York: Doubleday, 1965).

The Poet Assassinated, trans. Ron Padgett (London: Hart-Davis, 1968).

Selected Writings, trans. Roger Shattuck (New York: New Directions, 1971).

Zone, trans. Samuel Beckett (Dublin: Dolman Press, 1972).

Biography and Criticism

ADÉMA, MARCEL, *Apollinaire* (London: William Heinemann, 1954). The most seriously researched biography.

DAVIES, MARGARET, *Apollinaire* (Edinburgh and London: Oliver and Boyd, 1964). Criticism and biography combined.

LITTLE, ROGER, *Guillaume Apollinaire* (Athlone French Poets; London: Athlone Press, 1976). A lively critical study. Brief discussion of *Tiresias*.

STEEGMULLER, FRANCIS, *Apollinaire, Poet Among the Painters* (Harmondsworth: Penguin, 1973). Fascinatingly readable biography.

1

A CHRONOLOGY OF
MAURICE MAETERLINCK

1862   29 August, Mauritius Polydorus Maria Bernardus Maeterlinck born in the historic city of Ghent, Belgium, third of four children. His father is a retired notary, his mother a lawyer's daughter. Both are of Flemish stock.

1868–74   Conventional religious primary education. Summers spent in a country house surrounded by canals. As a child, narrowly escapes drowning. Writes comedies imitating Molière.

1874–81   Educated at Jesuit College of Sainte-Barbe—a harsh and ugly institution. Traumatized there by fearful accounts of sin and damnation, and left with lasting distaste for organized religion. But meets two kindred spirits, Charles Van Lerberghe and Grégoire Le Roy, interested in literary world.

1881–5   Obliged to study law at Ghent University by his authoritarian father, though already keen to write. Passes exams and qualifies by learning by rote.

1883   Publishes his first poem.

1885   Visits Paris, ostensibly to broaden his legal education. Strongly influenced by Impressionist painters and symbolist poets (Mallarmé, Laforgue, etc.). Befriended by the writers Villiers de l'Isle Adam and Joris Karl Huysmans. Dutifully returns to Ghent to practise law.

1889   First book of poems, *Serres chaudes* (*Hothouses*), published. First play, *La Princesse Maleine* (*Princess Maleine*), a dramatized fairy-tale, is a success. Gives up the law.

1891   *L'Intruse* (*The Intruder*) (masked actors play out man's rite of passage) performed at Paul Fort's Théâtre d'art. 11 December, *Les Aveugles* (*The Blind*) performed at Fort's theatre. Well received by the symbolists, but booed by the audience, who sneer at the pretentiousness of spraying the theatre with perfume to make the atmosphere more Baudelairean, and at the mismanagement of the dog, visibly pulled along by his collar. Writes *Les Sept Princesses* (*The Seven Princesses*), a despairing fairy-tale.

1893   *Pelleas and Melisande* performed. A dreamy, mysterious play, turned into an opera by Debussy the same year.

1894   Writes three plays for marionettes which emphasize man's passivity before his destiny. Visits England. Lionized by English, admired by Shaw and Yeats.

1895   Falls in love with a married actress of culture and charm, Georgette Leblanc, and definitively moves to Paris to live with her.

1896   Publishes a volume of essays, *Le Trésor des humbles* (*The Treasury of the Humble*). Writes *Aglavaine and Selysette*, a mystical play about the eternal triangle.

1901   Writes a scientific essay, *La vie des abeilles* (*The Life of the Bee*). *Ariane et Barbe-bleu* (*Ariadne and Bluebeard*), a feminist version of *Bluebeard*, in which Ariadne liberates herself from his tyranny.

1902–3 Plays about women: *Sœur Béatrice* (*Sister Beatrice*), a miracle play, *Mona Vanna*, set in fifteenth-century Venice, and *Joyzelle*, a medieval play about Merlin.

1904   *Le Double Jardin* (*The Double Garden*), an essay about nature.

1905   Writes *L'Oiseau bleu* (*The Blue Bird*), a play for children about a magical search for happiness, directed by Stanislavski in Moscow in 1909.

1906   Buys a villa in Grasse, where he writes his essay, *L'Intelligence des fleurs* (*The Intelligence of Flowers*). Hires a medieval abbey in Normandy for the summers. Suffers from writer's block and depression.

1908   Writes a play, *Mary Magdalene*; not a success.

1909   His translation of *Macbeth* performed in his abbey, with the actors and audience moving from room to room.

1910   Meets a young actress, Renée Dahon. Moves to the hills above Nice.

1911   Wins the Nobel Prize for Literature, 'on account of his diverse literary activity, and especially his dramatic works'.

1913   His essay *La Mort* (*Death*) placed on the Index by the Catholic Church, since it rejects formal Christianity.

1914   First World War: Maeterlinck an active supporter of Belgium. A new vein of robust realism in his propaganda articles and speeches.

1917   *Le Bourgmestre de Stilemonde* (*The Burgomaster of Stilemonde*), a propaganda play.

1919   Final separation from Georgette, and marriage to Renée Dahon. Visits New York, is lionized. Abortive attempt to hire him to write film scripts in Hollywood.

1920   Decorated with Grande Croix de l'Ordre de Léopold in Belgium.

1921   *Le Grand Secret* (*The Great Secret*), a history of the occult sciences.

1922   *Les Fiançailles* (*The Betrothal*), sequel to *The Blue Bird*, featuring the same hero's search for a bride.

1927–42 Twelve volumes of essays on scientific, mystical, and occult topics.

1932   Ennobled as Count Maeterlinck by the King of Belgium.

1935   *La Princesse Isabelle*, play about the curing of a young sick girl.

1939–47 Settles in Portugal to avoid the German occupation (he had been outspokenly anti-German during the 1914–18 war).

1940   Moves to New York for the same reason. Last plays are more positive about religion.

1947   Returns to Nice. Awarded a medal by the Académie française (he cannot be made a member as he is Belgian).

1949   Dies of a heart attack. Agnostic funeral.

A CHRONOLOGY OF ALFRED JARRY

1873   8 Sept., Alfred-Henri-Marie Jarry born in Laval (Loire). His father a prosperous cloth merchant, his mother an aristocrat—they lead virtually separate lives. Father soon loses his money.

1879–88   Educated at the Lycée of Saint-Brieuc. An excellent pupil. Writes early verse dramas, violent and morbid.

1888   Moves to Rennes. Educated at the lycée. His physics teacher is M. Hébert, the original of Ubu. His schoolfriends Charles and Henri Morin have already begun a cycle of writings about Hébert. Jarry collaborates with them. Dec., the boys stage *Les Polonais* (*The Poles*), a first version of *Ubu roi* (*Ubu the King*), using puppets, in the Morins' attic.

1891   Moves to Paris. Jarry attends lycée.

1892   Meets the poet Léon-Paul Fargue. Begins to move in literary circles.

1893   Publishes his first poem in a weekly literary magazine, *L'Echo de Paris*.

1894   First collective volume appears, *Les Minutes de sable mémorial* (*The Minutes of the Sand of Memory*), published by *Mercure de France*. It includes a piece about Ubu, 'Punch'. Joins literary circle run by his publisher's wife. Meets Valéry, Gide, Ravel, etc. Rousseau paints him. Reads *Ubu the King* to an audience of friends. Using legacy from his mother, starts an art magazine, *L'Ymagier*, which has seven issues. Also starts to drink very heavily. Together with opium abuse, this will contribute to his early death. Called up for national service.

1895   Discharged from the army on grounds of ill health. September, first version of *Ubu the King* published, *L'Acte terrestre de César-Antéchrist* (*The Terrestrial Act of Caesar Antichrist*).

1896   Meets Lugné-Poe, director of the Théâtre de l'Œuvre, and writes to him about Ubu. *Ubu the King* published twice more in 1896; also *Ubu cocu* (*Ubu Cuckold*). Publishes article 'On the Uselessness of Theatre' in the *Mercure de France*. *Ubu the King* staged in Lugné-Poe's theatre on 9 December. Jarry has organized the whole event, including the costumes, the casting, and the actors' tone of voice. The first night is a scandal, the public outraged. The critics are divided. From then on, Jarry adopts the personality of Ubu, and talks, reasons, and behaves like him (this is particularly incongruous as Jarry is diminutive in size).

1896–   Jarry grows increasingly eccentric, attending Mallarmé's funeral in bright yellow shoes, shooting at people in cafés, cycling everywhere, and often short of food.

1897   Publishes a novel about his time in the army, *Les Jours et les nuits: Roman d'un déserteur* (*Days and Nights: A Deserter's Novel*).

1898   *Ubu the King* performed, using puppets designed by the painter Bonnard. Completes *Gestes et opinions du docteur Faustroll, pataphysicien* (*The Deeds and Opinions of Doctor Faustroll, Pataphysician*), a 'neo-scientific novel'—published posthumously in 1911. *L'Almanach du Père Ubu illustré* (*The Illustrated Almanac of Père Ubu*).

1899   *Ubu enchaîné* (*Ubu Bound*), the final Ubu play.

1901   A second Ubu almanac published. *Messalina*, a novel set in ancient Rome. A puppet version of *Ubu sur la butte* (*Ubu on the Mound*), abridged from *Ubu the King*, put on.

1902   *Le Surmâle* (*The Supermale*), a science fiction novel about a sexual record-beater.

1905   An operetta, *Le Manoir enchanté* (*The Enchanted Manor*), performed privately.

1906   Jarry suffers a severe stroke.

1907   *Le Moutardier du Pape* (*The Pope's Mustard-Pot*) published, but fails to attract interest. 1 November, death from tuberculous meningitis.

A CHRONOLOGY OF
GUILLAUME APOLLINAIRE

1880   26 August, Rome: Birth of Wilhelm Albert Wladimir Alex-
        andre Apollinaris de Kostrowitzky, illegitimate son of a wild
        young Polish lady, Angelica de Kostrowitzky. His father is
        almost certainly an Italian officer, Francesco Flugi
        D'Aspremont (though Apollinaire later hints at a papal
        dignitary, and even at the son of Napoleon, as possible
        fathers).

1882   Apollinaire's brother Albert born.

1885–99 Abandoned by the children's father, Angelica settles on the
        Côte d'Azur, where she frequents the casinos and finds
        'protectors'. Apollinaire attends Catholic schools in Mon-
        aco, Cannes, and Nice.

1899   The family move to Paris. Apollinaire rapidly embarks on a
        writing career, most other avenues being closed to him
        because of his foreign nationality. His first published work
        is a pornographic pot-boiler, *Mirely ou le petit trou pas cher*
        (*Mirely or the Cheap Little Hole*).

1901–2 Employed as tutor on the banks of the Rhine to the daughter
        of a German noblewoman, Viscountess Milhau. Falls in
        love with the English governess, Annie Playden. Writes his
        first great poems, *Rhénanes* (*Rhineland Poems*), to her. She
        rejects his advances.

1902   Back in Paris, works in a bank; co-founder of a literary
        review, *Festin d'Ésope* (*Aesop's Feast*).

1903–8 Café society. Meets Picasso, Braque, Vlaminck, Derain,
        Matisse, Rousseau, and other painters; writes articles on
        many of them, and some of them paint or draw him. Meets

writers Max Jacob, Alfred Jarry, and others. Starts the literary–artistic collaboration that is to become his trademark as a critic. Writes reviews, essays, poems, and two erotic novels.

1908   Meets the painter Marie Laurencin. Their liaison is to last for six stormy years. Writes some of his finest poetry for her (e.g. 'Sous le pont Mirabeau').

1909   Agrees to edit a series of pornographic texts, with erudite introductions, which provides him with a regular income. Writes articles on literary figures, including a major piece on Jarry: 'His smallest actions, his pranks, everything was literature.' Publication of 'La Chanson du mal-aimé' ('The Song of the Unloved One'), a long poem written to Annie Playden.

1910   A volume of collected stories, *L'Hérésiarque et Cie* (*The Héresiarch and Company*), published. Regular art critic for *L'Intransigeant*.

1911   Regular columnist for *Mercure de France*—anecdotal accounts of painters, etc. Theft of the *Mona Lisa* from the Louvre. Apollinaire wrongly suspected and briefly imprisoned. Depressed and traumatized, and his reputation suffers.

1912   Associate editor of a new review, *Soirées de Paris*. Defends modern art, and is largely responsible for unifying the cubists into a movement. Publishes his great poem 'Zone'.

1913   Publishes his major poetry to date in one volume: *Alcools*. At the proofs stage, deletes all punctuation. His work criticized for resembling a junk shop.

1914   First World War: Apollinaire desperate to enlist. Finally accepted despite his foreign nationality.

1915   Promoted to officer. Despite a recent passionate affair with Louise de Coligny-Châtillon, becomes engaged to Madeleine Pagès, whom he had met on a train. Experiences trench warfare.

1916   17 March, wounded in the head by a shell-fragment. Trepanning operation—said to cause a personality change. He repudiates his fiancée, and reappears in Paris with a bandaged head. Publishes *Le Poète assassiné* (*The Assassinated Poet*), a collection of stories and pieces.

1917   Resumes literary life in Paris, contributing to poetry reviews. Writes the programme notes for Cocteau's ballet *Parade*, which he describes as 'a sort of sur-realism'—the first use of the word. 21 June, *Les Mamelles de Tirésias* (*The Mammaries of Tiresias*) performed for the first time. The first—and only—night is a scandal. The play is regarded as offensive and frivolous by traditionalists, hotly defended by modernists.

1918   Composes the preface to his play for publication. Publishes *Calligrammes*, visual poems in which the shape of the text on the page echoes the meaning. 2 May, marries Jacqueline Kolb. 9 November, weakened by his war wound, Apollinaire dies of Spanish flu.

THE BLIND

by

Maurice Maeterlinck

▬▬▬

*For Charles Van Lerberghe**

CHARACTERS

THE PRIEST*

THREE MEN BORN BLIND

THE OLDEST BLIND MAN

THE FIFTH BLIND MAN

THE SIXTH BLIND MAN

THREE OLD BLIND WOMEN AT PRAYER

THE OLDEST BLIND WOMAN

A YOUNG BLIND GIRL

A MAD BLIND WOMAN

THE BLIND

A very ancient Northern forest, with an eternal look to it beneath a sky thick with stars.—Centre stage, and in the deepest shadows, is seated an ancient PRIEST, wrapped in an ample black robe. His head and torso, tilted back a little and deathly still, are leaning against the trunk of an enormous hollow oak. His face, with its violet lips parted, is of a changeless waxen pallor. His expressionless staring eyes no longer look at the visible world this side of eternity, and the experience of endless grief and tears seems to have made them bloodshot. His hair, of the purest white, falls in straight, sparse locks over his face, which seems wiser and more weary than all that surrounds him in the watchful silence of the dreary forest. His wasted hands are rigidly clasped in his lap.—On the right, SIX BLIND OLD MEN are seated on stones, tree-stumps, and dead leaves. —On the left, separated from them by a fallen tree and blocks of stone, SIX WOMEN, also blind, are sitting facing the old men. THE FIFTH, whose bearing suggests dumb lunacy, has a sleeping infant on her lap. The sixth is glowing with youth and her long hair flows over her whole body. Both the women and the old men are dressed in identical voluminous, dark-coloured garments. Most of them are waiting, with their elbows on their knees and their faces in their hands; and all of them seem to have lost the habit of making pointless gestures, and no longer turn their heads at the muffled, uneasy sounds of the Island. A clump of tall, sickly asphodels are in flower, close to the priest, in the darkness. It is extraordinarily dark, despite the moonlight which, here and there, manages to dispel the shadows from the leaves.

FIRST MAN BORN BLIND

Hasn't he come back yet?

SECOND MAN BORN BLIND

You woke me up!

THIRD MAN BORN BLIND

I was asleep too.

FIRST MAN BORN BLIND

Hasn't he come back yet?

SECOND MAN BORN BLIND

I can't hear anything coming.

THIRD MAN BORN BLIND

It's time to go back to the hospice.

FIRST MAN BORN BLIND

It would help to know where we are.

SECOND MAN BORN BLIND

It's got cold since he left.

THE OLDEST BLIND MAN

Does anyone know where we are?

THE OLDEST BLIND WOMAN

We were walking for ages; we must be miles from the hospice.

FIRST MAN BORN BLIND

Ah! are the women opposite?

THE OLDEST BLIND WOMAN

We're sitting opposite you.

FIRST MAN BORN BLIND

Wait a minute, I'll come over to you.

He gets up and gropes his way forward

—Where are you?—Say something, so I can hear where you are!

THE OLDEST BLIND WOMAN

We're here, sitting on some stones.

FIRST MAN BORN BLIND

He moves forward and bumps into the tree-trunk and the blocks of stone

There's something separating us...

SECOND MAN BORN BLIND

Better stay where we are!

THIRD MAN BORN BLIND

Where are you women sitting?—Do you want to come over to us?

THE OLDEST BLIND WOMAN

We're scared to get up!

THIRD MAN BORN BLIND

Why did he split us up?

FIRST MAN BORN BLIND

I can hear some of the women praying.

SECOND MAN BORN BLIND

Yes; the three old women are praying.

5

FIRST MAN BORN BLIND

This isn't the moment to be praying!

SECOND MAN BORN BLIND

You can pray later, back in the dormitory.

THE THREE OLD WOMEN *continue praying*

THIRD MAN BORN BLIND

Who's sitting beside me? I'd like to know.

SECOND MAN BORN BLIND

I think it's me.

They grope about them

THIRD MAN BORN BLIND

We can't seem to touch each other!

FIRST MAN BORN BLIND

Yes, but we're not far apart.

He gropes around him with his stick and knocks it against the fifth blind man, who gives a stifled groan

The fellow who's hard of hearing is sitting beside us.

SECOND MAN BORN BLIND

I can't hear everybody. There were six of us just now.

FIRST MAN BORN BLIND

I'm just beginning to realize. Let's ask the women as well. We need to know what's going on. I can still hear the old women praying; are they sitting together?

6

THE OLDEST BLIND WOMAN

They're sitting beside me on a rock.

FIRST MAN BORN BLIND

I'm sitting on some dead leaves!

THIRD MAN BORN BLIND

And the beautiful blind girl, where's she?

THE OLDEST BLIND WOMAN

She's beside the women praying.

SECOND MAN BORN BLIND

Where's the madwoman and her baby?

THE YOUNG BLIND GIRL

He's asleep: don't wake him up!

FIRST MAN BORN BLIND

Oh! You're so far away from us! I thought you were opposite me!

THIRD MAN BORN BLIND

We know just about everything we need to know; let's have a chat till the priest gets back.

THE OLDEST BLIND WOMAN

He told us to wait in silence.

THIRD MAN BORN BLIND

We're not in a church.

THE OLDEST BLIND WOMAN

You don't know where we are.

7

THIRD MAN BORN BLIND

I get scared unless I talk.

SECOND MAN BORN BLIND

Do you know where the priest went?

THIRD MAN BORN BLIND

It seems to me he's left us alone too long.

FIRST MAN BORN BLIND

He's getting too old. I gather he hasn't been able to see for some time himself. He won't admit it, he's afraid someone else may come to look after us instead of him; but it's my belief he can scarcely see at all. We need a new guide; he doesn't listen to us any more, and there are too many of us. Nobody can see in the whole house except him and the three nuns; and they're all older than he is!—I'm sure he's got us all lost, and he's looking for the way back. Where's he gone?—He's no right to leave us here...

THE OLDEST BLIND MAN

He's gone a long way off; I think he had a serious talk with the women.

FIRST MAN BORN BLIND

He only ever talks to the women.—Don't we count any longer?— It's high time we made a complaint.

THE OLDEST BLIND MAN

Who would you complain to?

FIRST MAN BORN BLIND

I don't know yet; we shall see; we shall see.—But where's he gone? I'm asking the women.

THE OLDEST BLIND WOMAN

He was tired after the long walk. I think he sat down amongst us for a minute. He's been very sad and weak for the last few days. Since the doctor died he's been scared. He's all alone. He hardly ever speaks. I don't know what can have happened. He was determined to go out today. He said he wanted to see the Island one last time, in the sunshine, before winter came. I'm told winter will be very long and cold, and already the snows are coming from the North. He's been very worried; they say those big storms we've had recently have made the river rise, and all the dykes are giving way. And he said the sea frightened him; apparently the sea is rough and no one knows why, and the cliffs round the Island are just not high enough. He wanted to see for himself; but he hasn't told us what he's seen.—I think he's just gone to get some bread and water for the madwoman. He said he'd need to go a very long way... We'll just have to wait.

THE YOUNG BLIND GIRL

Just as he was leaving, he took my hands, and his hands were trembling as if he was afraid. Then he kissed me...

FIRST MAN BORN BLIND

Oh! Oh!

THE YOUNG BLIND GIRL

I asked him what had happened. He said he didn't know. He said that the reign of the old people was coming to an end, maybe...

FIRST MAN BORN BLIND

But what did he mean, when he said that?

THE YOUNG BLIND GIRL

I didn't understand him. He said he was going over by the lighthouse.

FIRST MAN BORN BLIND

Is there a lighthouse?

THE YOUNG BLIND GIRL

Yes, on the north side of the Island. I think we're quite close to it. He said he could see the beam shining right here, in the leaves. I've never known him sadder than today, and I think he's been crying for several days. I don't know why, but it made me cry too, though I couldn't see him. I didn't hear him leave. I stopped asking him questions. I could hear that he was smiling, but too gravely; I could hear that he was shutting his eyes and wanting to be quiet...

FIRST MAN BORN BLIND

He said nothing of all this to us!

THE YOUNG BLIND GIRL

When he speaks, you don't listen!

THE OLDEST BLIND WOMAN

You all mutter when he speaks.

SECOND MAN BORN BLIND

He simply said 'Good-night' as he went away.

THIRD MAN BORN BLIND

It must be very late.

FIRST MAN BORN BLIND

He said 'Good-night' once or twice as he went away, as if he were going to bed. I could hear him looking at me as he said

'Good-night, good-night!'—People's voices change when they're staring at someone.

THE FIFTH BLIND MAN

Take pity on those who cannot see!

FIRST MAN BORN BLIND

Who made that meaningless remark?

SECOND MAN BORN BLIND

I think it's the fellow who's hard of hearing.

FIRST MAN BORN BLIND

Be quiet!—This is no time for begging.

THIRD MAN BORN BLIND

Where did he go to find bread and water?

THE OLDEST BLIND WOMAN

He went off towards the sea.

THIRD MAN BORN BLIND

People shouldn't go to the seaside at his age!

SECOND MAN BORN BLIND

Are we near the sea?

THE OLDEST BLIND WOMAN

Yes; keep quiet a minute: you'll be able to hear it.

Close by, a calm sea can be heard murmuring against the cliffs

SECOND MAN BORN BLIND

I can hear nothing but the three old women praying.

The Blind

THE OLDEST BLIND WOMAN

Listen carefully, you'll hear it through their prayers.

SECOND MAN BORN BLIND

Yes; I can hear something not far from here.

THE OLDEST BLIND MAN

The sea was sleeping; it seems it's waking up.

FIRST MAN BORN BLIND

He did wrong bringing us here; I don't like hearing that sound.

THE OLDEST BLIND MAN

You know very well the Island isn't very big; you can hear it the moment you get outside the hospice walls.

SECOND MAN BORN BLIND

I've never listened to it before.

THIRD MAN BORN BLIND

Today it feels as though it's right beside us; I don't like hearing it so close.

SECOND MAN BORN BLIND

I don't either; besides, we didn't ask to leave the hospice.

THIRD MAN BORN BLIND

We've never come as far as this; there was no point bringing us so far.

THE OLDEST BLIND WOMAN

It was beautiful weather this morning; he wanted us to enjoy the last few sunny days, before we were shut up in the hospice for the whole winter.

FIRST MAN BORN BLIND

But I'd rather stay in the hospice!

THE OLDEST BLIND WOMAN

Another thing he said was that we ought to get to know this little Island, since we live on it. Even he hasn't been all over it; there's a mountain no one's climbed, and valleys where people don't like going, and caves that nobody's ever explored. And he said it was a bad thing to stay in the dormitory, under the vaulted ceiling, waiting for the sun to shine; he wanted to take us to the sea-shore. But now he's gone there alone.

THE OLDEST BLIND MAN

He's right; we must think about living.

FIRST MAN BORN BLIND

But there's nothing to see out of doors!

SECOND MAN BORN BLIND

Are we in the sunshine right now?

THE SIXTH BLIND MAN

I don't think so; it seems very late to me.

SECOND MAN BORN BLIND

What time is it?

THE OTHER BLIND PEOPLE

I don't know.—Nobody knows.

SECOND MAN BORN BLIND

Is it still daylight?

To the sixth blind man

—Where are you?—Let's see; you can see a bit, so let's see!

THE SIXTH BLIND MAN

I think it's very dark; when we're in the sunshine, I can see a blue line under my eyelids; I did see one, ages ago, but right now I can see nothing.

FIRST MAN BORN BLIND

Well, I know it's late when I'm hungry, and I am hungry.

THIRD MAN BORN BLIND

Look up at the sky; maybe you'll see something!

They all lift their heads towards the sky, except for THE THREE MEN BORN BLIND, *who go on looking down at the ground*

THE SIXTH BLIND MAN

I don't know if we're out in the open.

FIRST MAN BORN BLIND

Our voices are hollow as if we were in a cave.

THE OLDEST BLIND MAN

No, I think they sound hollow because it's night-time.

THE YOUNG BLIND GIRL

I believe I can feel the moonlight on my hands.

THE OLDEST BLIND WOMAN

I think the stars are out; I can hear them.

THE YOUNG BLIND GIRL

Me too.

The Blind

FIRST MAN BORN BLIND

I can't hear anything.

SECOND MAN BORN BLIND

I can just hear us breathing!

THE OLDEST BLIND MAN

I think the women are right.

FIRST MAN BORN BLIND

I've never heard the stars.

THE TWO OTHER MEN BORN BLIND

Nor have we.

A flock of night birds suddenly lands in the leafy branches

SECOND MAN BORN BLIND

Listen to that! Listen to that!—What's that over our heads?—
Did you hear it?

THE OLDEST BLIND MAN

Something passed between the sky and us!

FIRST MAN BORN BLIND

I don't know what sort of noise that was.—I want to go home
to the hospice.

SECOND MAN BORN BLIND

We need to know where we are!

THE SIXTH BLIND MAN

I tried to get up; there's nothing but thorns all around me; I
don't dare stretch out my hands.

THIRD MAN BORN BLIND

We need to know where we are!

THE OLDEST BLIND MAN

There's no way of knowing!

THE SIXTH BLIND MAN

We must be very far from home; I can't understand any of the sounds here.

THIRD MAN BORN BLIND

I've been smelling the smell of dead leaves for ages!

THE SIXTH BLIND MAN

Does anyone remember seeing the Island in the past, and can they tell us where we are?

THE OLDEST BLIND WOMAN

We were all blind by the time we got here.

FIRST MAN BORN BLIND

We've never been able to see.

SECOND MAN BORN BLIND

Don't let's worry over nothing; he'll be back soon; let's go on waiting; but in future, don't let's allow him to take us out.

THE OLDEST BLIND MAN

We can't go out on our own.

FIRST MAN BORN BLIND

We won't go out any more, I'd rather not go out.

SECOND MAN BORN BLIND

We never wanted to go out, nobody asked to go out.

THE OLDEST BLIND WOMAN

It was a festival day on the Island; we always go out for the important festivals.

THIRD MAN BORN BLIND

He came and tapped me on the shoulder while I was still asleep, and said: 'Get up, get up, it's time, the sun is high in the sky!'— Was that true? I didn't notice. I've never seen the sun.

THE OLDEST BLIND MAN

I've seen the sun, when I was very young.

THE OLDEST BLIND WOMAN

Me too, years ago; when I was a little girl; but I can scarcely remember it.

THIRD MAN BORN BLIND

Why does he want us to go out every time the sun shows its face? Which of us can tell the difference? When I'm out for a walk, I never know if it's midday or midnight.

THE SIXTH BLIND MAN

I'd rather go out at midday; I get a feeling that everything's very bright then; and my eyes try very hard to open.

THIRD MAN BORN BLIND

I'd rather stay in the refectory, by the blazing coal-fire; we had a good fire going this morning...

SECOND MAN BORN BLIND

He could have taken us as far as the courtyard to sit in the sun; we're sheltered by the walls there; you can't wander out, there's nothing to be afraid of, so long as the door is shut;— I always shut it myself.—Why are you nudging my left elbow?

FIRST MAN BORN BLIND

I never touched you; I can't reach you.

SECOND MAN BORN BLIND

I tell you someone touched my elbow!

FIRST MAN BORN BLIND

It's not one of us.

THE OLDEST BLIND WOMAN

Oh God! Oh God! Tell us where we are!

FIRST MAN BORN BLIND

We can't wait here for ever!

Very far away a clock can be heard striking twelve, very slowly

THE OLDEST BLIND WOMAN

Oh! How far we are from the hospice!

THE OLDEST BLIND MAN

It's midnight!

SECOND MAN BORN BLIND

It's midday!—Does anyone know which?—Tell us!

THE SIXTH BLIND MAN

I don't know; but I think we're in the shade.

FIRST MAN BORN BLIND

I can't work things out; we've been asleep for too long.

SECOND MAN BORN BLIND

I'm hungry!

THE OTHER BLIND PEOPLE

We're hungry and thirsty!

SECOND MAN BORN BLIND

Have we been here long?

THE OLDEST BLIND WOMAN

I feel as if I've been here for centuries!

THE SIXTH BLIND MAN

I'm beginning to realize where we are...

THIRD MAN BORN BLIND

We'll have to go towards the bell that struck midnight...

Suddenly, all the night-birds give a triumphant call in the darkness

FIRST MAN BORN BLIND

Did you hear that? Did you hear that?

SECOND MAN BORN BLIND

Aren't we alone here?

THIRD MAN BORN BLIND

I've had my doubts for some time; someone's listening.—Is he back yet?

FIRST MAN BORN BLIND

I don't know what it was; it came from above our heads.

SECOND MAN BORN BLIND

Didn't the others hear anything?—You never say a word!

THE OLDEST BLIND MAN

We're still listening.

THE YOUNG BLIND GIRL

I can hear wings around me!

THE OLDEST BLIND WOMAN

Oh God! Oh God! Tell us where we are!

THE SIXTH BLIND MAN

I'm beginning to figure out where we are... The hospice is the other side of the great river; we've crossed the old bridge. He's led us to the north of the Island. We're not far from the river, and if we listen for a minute, we might hear it... If he doesn't come back, we'll have to go down to the water's edge. Big ships pass there, night and day, and the sailors will see us on the river-bank. We could be in the forest round the lighthouse; but I don't know the way out... Is anyone ready to follow me?

FIRST MAN BORN BLIND

Let's stay sitting here!—Let's wait, let's wait;—we don't know which way to go for the great river, and there are marshes all round the hospice; let's wait, let's wait... He'll come back; he's got to come back!

THE SIXTH BLIND MAN

Does anyone know which way we took to get here? He was explaining it as we were walking.

FIRST MAN BORN BLIND

I didn't take any notice.

THE SIXTH BLIND MAN

Did anyone listen to him?

THIRD MAN BORN BLIND

We'll have to listen to him in future.

THE SIXTH BLIND MAN

Was any one of us born on the Island?

THE OLDEST BLIND MAN

You know very well that we've all come from elsewhere.

THE OLDEST BLIND WOMAN

We come from across the sea.

FIRST MAN BORN BLIND

During the crossing, I thought I was going to die.

SECOND MAN BORN BLIND

Me too;—we came over together.

THIRD MAN BORN BLIND

We all three come from the same parish.

FIRST MAN BORN BLIND

They say you can see it from here, when the weather is clear;—over to the north.—It hasn't got a steeple.

THIRD MAN BORN BLIND

It was pure chance we landed here.

THE OLDEST BLIND WOMAN

I come from somewhere quite different...

SECOND MAN BORN BLIND

Where are you from?

THE OLDEST BLIND WOMAN

I don't like to think about it any more... I can scarcely remember anything when I talk about it... It's too long ago... It was colder there than it is here.

THE YOUNG BLIND GIRL

I come from very far away...

FIRST MAN BORN BLIND

So where are you from?

THE YOUNG BLIND GIRL

I couldn't say. How could I explain?—It's too far from here, way across the sea. I come from a big country... I could only show you by making signs; but we can't see any more... I've been a wanderer for too long... But I've seen the sun, and water and fire, and mountains and faces and strange flowers... There's nothing like them on this Island; it's too dark and too cold here... Since I've been blind, I've never smelt their scent... But I have seen my parents and my sisters... I was too young then to know where I was... I used to play by the seaside... But how well I remember seeing!... One day, I was at the top of a mountain looking at the snow... I was beginning to see which people would end up unhappy...

FIRST MAN BORN BLIND

What do you mean?

THE YOUNG BLIND GIRL

Sometimes I can still tell it by their voices... Some of my memories are clearer when I don't think about them...

FIRST MAN BORN BLIND

I don't have any memories, myself...

A flock of big migratory birds flies over, calling, above the leaves

THE OLDEST BLIND MAN

Something else is passing under the sky!

22

SECOND MAN BORN BLIND

Why did you come here?

THE OLDEST BLIND MAN

Who are you talking to?

SECOND MAN BORN BLIND

Our young sister.

THE YOUNG BLIND GIRL

They told me he'd be able to cure me. He says I'll be able to see one day. Then I can leave the Island.

FIRST MAN BORN BLIND

We all want to leave the Island!

SECOND MAN BORN BLIND

We'll all stay here for ever!

THIRD MAN BORN BLIND

He's too old; he won't have time to cure us!

THE YOUNG BLIND GIRL

My eyelids are closed, but I can feel my eyes are alive...

FIRST MAN BORN BLIND

Mine are open.

SECOND MAN BORN BLIND

I sleep with my eyes open.

THIRD MAN BORN BLIND

Let's not keep talking about our eyes!

SECOND MAN BORN BLIND

You haven't been here long, have you?

THE OLDEST BLIND MAN

One night, at prayer time, among the women, I heard a voice I didn't recognize; and I could hear from your voice you were very young... Hearing your voice, I'd have liked to see you as well...

FIRST MAN BORN BLIND

I never noticed.

THE SIXTH BLIND MAN

They say you're beautiful, like the women from far away.

THE YOUNG BLIND GIRL

I've never seen myself.

THE OLDEST BLIND MAN

We've never seen each other. We ask each other questions, and we answer them; we live together, we're always together, but we don't know what we are!... It's all very well to touch each other with our two hands, eyes can see better than hands.

THE SIXTH BLIND MAN

Sometimes when you're in the sunshine, I can see your shadows.

THE OLDEST BLIND MAN

We've never seen the house we live in; it's all very well to run our hands over the walls and the windows, we don't know where we live!...

THE OLDEST BLIND WOMAN

They say it's a very dark and gloomy old castle, no light ever shines there, except in the tower where the priest's room is.

FIRST MAN BORN BLIND

Those who can't see have no need of light.

THE SIXTH BLIND MAN

When I'm with the sheep, close by the hospice, they go home by themselves at night, when they see the light in that tower...
—They've never led me astray.

THE OLDEST BLIND MAN

We've been together for years and years, and we've never had a sight of each other! It's as if we're always on our own... You can't love someone without seeing them...

THE YOUNG BLIND GIRL

Sometimes I dream I can see...

THE OLDEST BLIND MAN

I only see in my dreams.

FIRST MAN BORN BLIND

Normally I only dream at midnight.

A gust of wind shakes the forest, and the leaves fall in dark masses

THE FIFTH BLIND MAN

Who's that touching my hands?

FIRST MAN BORN BLIND

Something's falling all around us!

THE OLDEST BLIND MAN

It comes from up there; I don't know what it is...

THE FIFTH BLIND MAN

Who's that touching my hands? I was asleep; let me sleep!

THE OLDEST BLIND MAN

Nobody's been touching your hands.

THE FIFTH BLIND MAN

Who's that taking my hands? Speak up when you answer, I'm a bit hard of hearing...

THE OLDEST BLIND MAN

We don't know any more than you do.

THE FIFTH BLIND MAN

Has anyone come to tell us what's going on?

FIRST MAN BORN BLIND

There's no point answering; he can't hear a thing.

THIRD MAN BORN BLIND

You must admit, deaf people are very unfortunate.

THE OLDEST BLIND MAN

I'm tired of sitting down!

THE SIXTH BLIND MAN

I'm tired of being here!

SECOND MAN BORN BLIND

I feel as if we're all too far apart... let's try to get closer together;—it's beginning to feel cold...

THIRD MAN BORN BLIND

I don't dare get up! Better stay where we are.

THE OLDEST BLIND MAN

You never know what there might be between us.

THE SIXTH BLIND MAN

I believe both my hands are bleeding; I was trying to get up.

THIRD MAN BORN BLIND

I can hear you leaning towards me.

THE BLIND MADWOMAN, *groaning, rubs her eyes violently, turning persistently towards the motionless priest*

FIRST MAN BORN BLIND

I can hear yet another sound...

THE OLDEST BLIND WOMAN

I think it's our poor sister rubbing her eyes.

SECOND MAN BORN BLIND

That's all she ever does; I hear her every night.

THIRD MAN BORN BLIND

She's mad; she never says a word.

THE OLDEST BLIND WOMAN

She hasn't spoken since she had the baby... She always seems scared...

THE OLDEST BLIND MAN

Aren't you scared in this place?

FIRST MAN BORN BLIND

Which of us?

27

THE OLDEST BLIND MAN

The whole lot of you!

THE OLDEST BLIND WOMAN

Yes, yes, we're scared all right!

THE YOUNG BLIND GIRL

We've been scared for ages!

FIRST MAN BORN BLIND

Why did you ask that question?

THE OLDEST BLIND MAN

I don't know why I asked... Suddenly I think I can hear one of us crying!...

FIRST MAN BORN BLIND

You mustn't be afraid; I think it's the madwoman...

THE OLDEST BLIND MAN

There's something else as well...

THE OLDEST BLIND WOMAN

She always cries when it's time to put the baby to the breast.

FIRST MAN BORN BLIND

She's the only one who cries like that!

THE OLDEST BLIND WOMAN

They say there are moments when she can still see...

FIRST MAN BORN BLIND

You never hear the others crying...

THE OLDEST BLIND MAN

You have to see to cry...

28

THE YOUNG BLIND GIRL

I can smell the scent of flowers around us...

FIRST MAN BORN BLIND

All I can smell is the smell of earth!

THE YOUNG BLIND GIRL

There are flowers, there are flowers around us!

SECOND MAN BORN BLIND

All I can smell is the smell of earth!

THE OLDEST BLIND WOMAN

I smelt the scent of flowers on the wind...

THIRD MAN BORN BLIND

All I can smell is the smell of earth!

THE OLDEST BLIND MAN

I believe the women are right.

THE SIXTH BLIND MAN

Where are they?—I'll go and pick them.

THE YOUNG BLIND GIRL

On your right. Get up.

THE SIXTH BLIND MAN *gets up slowly and gropes his way forwards, bumping into bushes and trees, towards the asphodels which he knocks over and tramples as he passes*

THE YOUNG BLIND GIRL

I can hear you breaking the living stems! Stop, stop!

FIRST MAN BORN BLIND

Stop fussing about the flowers, and give some thought to getting back!

THE SIXTH BLIND MAN

I don't dare go back the way I came!

THE YOUNG BLIND GIRL

There's no need to come back.—Wait there.

She gets up

—Oh! How cold the ground is! There's going to be a frost.

She moves forward without hesitating towards the strange pale asphodels, but she is stopped by the fallen tree and the blocks of stone, near the flowers

—They're over here!—I can't reach them; they're over on your side.

THE SIXTH BLIND MAN

I'm picking them, I think.

Groping, he picks up the scattered flowers, and offers them to her; the night-birds fly away

THE YOUNG BLIND GIRL

I believe I saw flowers like these, long ago... I can't remember their name... How sickly they are, and how limp their stems are! They're almost unrecognizable... I think they're the flowers of the dead...*

She plaits asphodels in her hair

30

THE OLDEST BLIND MAN

I can hear the sound of your hair.

THE YOUNG BLIND GIRL

That's the flowers.

THE OLDEST BLIND MAN

We'll never see each other...

THE YOUNG BLIND GIRL

I'll never see myself either... I'm cold.

At that moment, the wind rises in the forest, and suddenly and violently the sea booms against the cliffs. It sounds very close

FIRST MAN BORN BLIND

It's thundering!

SECOND MAN BORN BLIND

I think a storm is brewing.

THE OLDEST BLIND WOMAN

I think it's the sea.

THIRD MAN BORN BLIND

The sea?—Is it the sea?—But then it's very close to us!—Right next to us! I can hear it all around me!—It's got to be something else!

THE YOUNG BLIND GIRL

I can hear the sound of the waves at my feet.

FIRST MAN BORN BLIND

I think it's the wind in the dead leaves.

31

THE OLDEST BLIND MAN

I think the women are right.

THIRD MAN BORN BLIND

It will reach us here!

FIRST MAN BORN BLIND

Where's the wind coming from?

SECOND MAN BORN BLIND

It comes from the sea.

THE OLDEST BLIND MAN

It always comes from the sea; the sea's all around us. It can't come from anywhere else...

FIRST MAN BORN BLIND

Don't let's go on thinking about the sea!

SECOND MAN BORN BLIND

But we've got to think about it, because it's going to get to us!

FIRST MAN BORN BLIND

You can't be sure it is the sea...

SECOND MAN BORN BLIND

I can hear the waves, so close I could dip my hands in! We mustn't stay here! The waves could be all around us!

THE OLDEST BLIND MAN

Where do you suggest we go?

SECOND MAN BORN BLIND

Anywhere! Anywhere! I don't want to go on hearing the sound of the water! Let's go away! Let's go away!

THIRD MAN BORN BLIND

I think I can hear something else.—Listen!

The sound of rapid footsteps through the dead leaves is heard in the distance

FIRST MAN BORN BLIND

Something's coming!

SECOND MAN BORN BLIND

He's coming! He's coming! He's coming back!

THIRD MAN BORN BLIND

He's taking tiny steps, like a small child...

SECOND MAN BORN BLIND

Let's not tell him what we think of him, not today!

THE OLDEST BLIND WOMAN

I don't believe those are a man's footsteps!

A big dog* enters the forest, and passes in front of the blind people.—Silence

FIRST MAN BORN BLIND

Who's there?—Who are you?—Have pity on us, we've been waiting so long!...

The dog stops and comes over to the blind man and puts its front paws on his knees

Ah! Ah! What have you put on my knees? What is it? Is it an animal?—I believe it's a dog?... Oh! Oh! It's the dog! It's the hospice dog! Come here! Come here! He's come to rescue us! Here, boy! Here, boy!

THE OTHER BLIND PEOPLE

Here, boy! Here, boy!

FIRST MAN BORN BLIND

He's come to rescue us! He's followed our trail as far as here. He's licking my hands as though we'd been apart for centuries!

THE OTHER BLIND PEOPLE

Here, boy! Here, boy!

THE OLDEST BLIND MAN

Could there be someone following him?

FIRST MAN BORN BLIND

No, no, he's on his own.— I can't hear anyone coming.— He's the only guide we need; we couldn't find a better one. He'll take us everywhere we want to go; he'll do as we tell him...

THE OLDEST BLIND WOMAN

I don't dare follow him.

THE YOUNG BLIND GIRL

Nor do I.

FIRST MAN BORN BLIND

Why not? He can see better than we can.

SECOND MAN BORN BLIND

Don't let's listen to the women.

THIRD MAN BORN BLIND

The sky seems different; I can breathe more easily; the air seems pure now...

THE OLDEST BLIND WOMAN

It's the sea-breeze blowing around us.

THE SIXTH BLIND MAN

I think it's going to be a clear day; I believe the sun's rising...

THE OLDEST BLIND WOMAN

I think it's turning cold...

FIRST MAN BORN BLIND

We'll find our way home. He's pulling me!... He's pulling me. He's beside himself with joy—I can't hold him back!... Follow me! Follow me! We're on our way home!...

He gets up, pulled by the dog, who takes him as far as the motionless priest, and stops

THE OTHER BLIND PEOPLE

Where are you? Where are you?—Where are you going?—Be careful!

FIRST MAN BORN BLIND

Hold on! Hold on! Don't follow me just yet; I'll come back... He's stopped.—What's the matter?—Ah! Ah! I'm touching something very cold!

SECOND MAN BORN BLIND

What are you saying? We can scarcely hear you.

FIRST MAN BORN BLIND

I've touched something! I think I'm touching a face!

35

THIRD MAN BORN BLIND

What's that?—We can't understand you. What's wrong?—
Where are you?—Have you moved away from us so quickly?

FIRST MAN BORN BLIND

Oh! Oh! Oh!—I don't understand this yet... —there's a dead
man among us!

THE OTHER BLIND PEOPLE

A dead man among us?—Where are you? Where are
you?

FIRST MAN BORN BLIND

There's a dead man among us, I tell you! Oh! Oh! I've touched
a dead man's face!—You're sitting next to a dead man! One of
us must have died suddenly! Come on, say something, I need to
know who's alive! Where are you all?—come on, answer me,
all of you!

THE BLIND PEOPLE *answer in turn, except the blind madwoman
and the deaf blind man;* THE THREE OLD WOMEN *have stopped
praying*

FIRST MAN BORN BLIND

I can't make out which is which!... You all sound the same!... All
your voices are quavering!

THIRD MAN BORN BLIND

Two of us didn't answer... Where are they?

He pokes at the fifth blind man with his stick

THE FIFTH BLIND MAN

Oh! Oh! I was asleep; let me sleep!

THE SIXTH BLIND MAN

It's not him.—Is it the madwoman?

THE OLDEST BLIND WOMAN

She's sitting beside me; I can hear she's alive.

FIRST MAN BORN BLIND

I believe... I believe it's the priest!—He's standing up! Come here! Come here! Come here!

SECOND MAN BORN BLIND

So he's not dead, then?

THE OLDEST BLIND MAN

Where is he?

THE SIXTH BLIND MAN

Let's go and see.

They all get up, except the madwoman and the fifth blind man, and grope their way forwards towards the dead man

SECOND MAN BORN BLIND

Is he here?—Is it him?

THIRD MAN BORN BLIND

Yes! Yes! I recognize him!

FIRST MAN BORN BLIND

Oh God! Oh God! What will become of us?

THE OLDEST BLIND WOMAN

Father, father, is it you? What's happened to you, father?— What's the matter with you?—Answer us!—We're all here, standing round you...

THE OLDEST BLIND MAN

Fetch some water; he could still be alive...

SECOND MAN BORN BLIND

Let's try to do something... Perhaps he could still lead us back to the hospice...

THIRD MAN BORN BLIND

It's no use; I can't hear a heartbeat.—He's stone cold...

FIRST MAN BORN BLIND

He died without saying a word.

THIRD MAN BORN BLIND

He might have warned us.

SECOND MAN BORN BLIND

Oh! How old he was!... I've never touched his face before...

THIRD MAN BORN BLIND

feeling the corpse

He's taller than we are!...

SECOND MAN BORN BLIND

His eyes are wide open; he died with his hands clasped...

FIRST MAN BORN BLIND

He died just like that, pointlessly...

SECOND MAN BORN BLIND

He's not standing up, he's sitting on a stone...

THE OLDEST BLIND WOMAN

Oh God! Oh God! I didn't know the whole story!... the whole story!... He'd been ill for so long... He must have suffered today!... —He never complained... except by clasping our hands... You can't always understand... You can't ever understand!... Let's all pray around him; down on your knees...

Groaning, THE WOMEN *go down on their knees*

FIRST MAN BORN BLIND

I don't dare kneel down...

SECOND MAN BORN BLIND

You never know what you may be kneeling on...

THIRD MAN BORN BLIND

Was he sick?... He never told us...

SECOND MAN BORN BLIND

I heard him talking in a low voice as he was leaving us... I think he was talking to our young sister; what did he say?

FIRST MAN BORN BLIND

She won't tell us.

SECOND MAN BORN BLIND

Won't you tell us?—Where are you?—Speak to us!

THE OLDEST BLIND WOMAN

You caused him too much pain; it's your fault he's dead... you didn't want to go on walking; you wanted to sit on the stony path instead, eating your provisions; you grumbled all day long... I could hear him sighing... He lost heart...

FIRST MAN BORN BLIND

Was he sick? Did you know about it?

THE OLDEST BLIND MAN

We didn't know a thing... We've never seen him... When have we ever known what's in front of our poor dead eyes?... He never complained... Now it's too late... I've seen three of them die... but never like this... Now it's our turn...

FIRST MAN BORN BLIND

It wasn't my fault he was suffering.—I never said a thing...

SECOND MAN BORN BLIND

Nor did I; we just followed him without a word...

THIRD MAN BORN BLIND

He died on his way to fetch water for the madwoman...

FIRST MAN BORN BLIND

What are we to do? Where are we to go?

THIRD MAN BORN BLIND

Where's the dog?

FIRST MAN BORN BLIND

Here; he doesn't want to leave the body.

THIRD MAN BORN BLIND

Drag him off! Pull him away! Pull him away!

FIRST MAN BORN BLIND

He doesn't want to leave the body.

SECOND MAN BORN BLIND

We can't stay here waiting round a dead body!... We can't die here in the dark!

THIRD MAN BORN BLIND

Let's stick together; don't let's get too far apart; let's hold hands, and all sit together on this stone... Where are the others?... Come here! Come on! Come on!

THE OLDEST BLIND MAN

Where are you?

THIRD MAN BORN BLIND

Here; I'm here. Are we all together?—Come closer.—Where are your hands?—It's very cold.

THE YOUNG BLIND GIRL

Oh! How cold your hands are!

THIRD MAN BORN BLIND

What are you doing?

THE YOUNG BLIND GIRL

I was putting my hands over my eyes; I felt as if I was suddenly going to be able to see...

FIRST MAN BORN BLIND

Who's that crying?

THE OLDEST BLIND WOMAN

It's the madwoman sobbing.

FIRST MAN BORN BLIND

Do you think she realizes?

THE OLDEST BLIND MAN

I think we're all going to die here...

41

The Blind

THE OLDEST BLIND WOMAN

Maybe someone will come...

FIRST MAN BORN BLIND

I expect the nuns will come out of the hospice...

THE OLDEST BLIND WOMAN

They never come out at night.

THE YOUNG BLIND GIRL

They never come out at all.

SECOND MAN BORN BLIND

I expect the lighthouse-keepers will notice us...

THE OLDEST BLIND MAN

They never leave their lighthouse.

THIRD MAN BORN BLIND

Perhaps they'll see us...

THE OLDEST BLIND WOMAN

They always look out over the sea.

THIRD MAN BORN BLIND

It's cold!

THE OLDEST BLIND MAN

Listen to the dead leaves; I think there's a frost.

THE YOUNG BLIND GIRL

Oh! How hard the ground is!

THIRD MAN BORN BLIND

I can hear a sound I don't understand, over there on my left...

THE OLDEST BLIND MAN

It's the sea roaring against the rocks.

THIRD MAN BORN BLIND

I thought it was the women.

THE OLDEST BLIND WOMAN

I can hear the ice cracking under the waves...

FIRST MAN BORN BLIND

Which of you is trembling like that? You're making us all shiver on this stone.

SECOND MAN BORN BLIND

My hands won't open any longer.

THE OLDEST BLIND MAN

I can hear another sound I don't understand...

FIRST MAN BORN BLIND

Which of you is trembling amongst us? You're making the whole stone shiver!

THE OLDEST BLIND MAN

I believe it's a woman.

THE OLDEST BLIND WOMAN

I think the madwoman's shivering the hardest.

THIRD MAN BORN BLIND

I can't hear her baby.

THE OLDEST BLIND WOMAN

I think he's still feeding.

THE OLDEST BLIND MAN

He's the only one who can see where we are!

FIRST MAN BORN BLIND

I can hear the North wind.

THE SIXTH BLIND MAN

I think the stars have all gone; we're going to have snow.

THIRD MAN BORN BLIND

If anyone falls asleep, we'll have to wake them up.

THE OLDEST BLIND MAN

But I do feel sleepy!

A gust of wind makes the dead leaves whirl

THE YOUNG BLIND GIRL

Can you hear the dead leaves?—I think someone's coming towards us...

SECOND MAN BORN BLIND

It's only the wind; listen!

THIRD MAN BORN BLIND

Nobody's ever going to come!

THE OLDEST BLIND MAN

The winter cold is going to come...

THE YOUNG BLIND GIRL

I can hear footsteps in the distance.

The Blind

FIRST MAN BORN BLIND

I can hear nothing but the dead leaves!

THE YOUNG BLIND GIRL

I can hear footsteps very far away!

SECOND MAN BORN BLIND

I can hear nothing but the North wind!

THE YOUNG BLIND GIRL

I tell you someone's coming this way!

THE OLDEST BLIND WOMAN

I can hear very slow footsteps...

THE OLDEST BLIND MAN

I believe the women are right!

Giant snowflakes begin to fall

FIRST MAN BORN BLIND

Oh! Oh! What are these cold things falling on my hands?

THE SIXTH BLIND MAN

It's snowing!

FIRST MAN BORN BLIND

Let's all huddle together.

THE YOUNG BLIND GIRL

Listen to the footsteps!

THE OLDEST BLIND WOMAN

For God's sake be quiet for a minute!

THE YOUNG BLIND GIRL

They're coming closer! They're coming closer! Do listen!

Suddenly the madwoman's baby begins to wail in the darkness

THE OLDEST BLIND MAN

Is the baby crying?

THE YOUNG BLIND GIRL

He can see! He can see! He must be seeing something if he's crying.

She snatches up the child and moves forward towards where the footsteps seem to be coming from; anxiously, the other women follow her and gather round her

I'm going to meet whatever it is.

THE OLDEST BLIND WOMAN

Be careful!

THE YOUNG BLIND GIRL

Oh! How hard he's crying!—What's the matter?—Don't cry.— Don't be afraid, there's nothing to be scared of, we're here; we're all around you.—What can you see?—Don't be scared.— Don't cry like that! What can you see?—Say, what can you see?

THE OLDEST BLIND WOMAN

The footsteps are coming this way; listen! just listen!

THE OLDEST BLIND MAN

I can hear a dress brushing against the dead leaves.

THE SIXTH BLIND MAN

Is it a woman?

THE OLDEST BLIND MAN

Is it the sound of footsteps?

FIRST MAN BORN BLIND

Could it be the sea in the dead leaves?

THE YOUNG BLIND GIRL

No, no! It's footsteps! It's footsteps! It's footsteps!

THE OLDEST BLIND WOMAN

We'll soon know; listen to the dead leaves rustling!

THE YOUNG BLIND GIRL

I can hear them, I can hear them, they've almost reached us! listen! listen!—What do you see? What do you see?

THE OLDEST BLIND WOMAN

Which way is he looking?

THE YOUNG BLIND GIRL

He keeps looking towards the footsteps!—See, see! When I turn him round, he turns back to look... He can see! He can see! He can see!—He must be seeing something strange!...

THE OLDEST BLIND WOMAN

Hold him up over our heads, so that he can look.

THE YOUNG BLIND GIRL

Keep back! Keep back!

She lifts the child high over the group of blind people

The Blind

—The footsteps have stopped right here among us...

THE OLDEST BLIND WOMAN

They're here! They're in our midst!...

THE YOUNG BLIND GIRL

Who are you?

Silence

THE OLDEST BLIND WOMAN

Have pity on us!

Silence—The child's wailing grows more frantic

THE END

UBU THE KING

by

Alfred Jarry

Portrait of Ubu the King by Jarry

THIS BOOK

is dedicated to

MARCEL SCHWOB*

Thereat Père Ubu shooke his noddle,* he who thereafter
was y-klept by ye English Shakspear, and by that name
hath given you manie a fair tragedie y-writ.

CHARACTERS*

Père UBU

Mère UBU

CAPTAIN BRUBBISH

KING WENCESLAS

QUEEN ROSEMONDE

BOLESLAS

LADISLAS ⎫ Their Sons

BUGGERLAS ⎭

GENERAL LASKY

STANISLAS LECZINSKY

JAN SOBIESKY

NICOLAS RENSKY

THE EMPEROR ALEXIS

GYRON

PILE ⎬ Pillodins

COTTISE

CONSPIRATORS AND SOLDIERS

POPULACE

MICHAEL FEDEROVITCH

NOBLES

MAGISTRATES

COUNCILLORS

FINANCIERS

MONEY-GRABBERS

PEASANTS
THE ENTIRE RUSSIAN ARMY
THE ENTIRE POLISH ARMY
Mère UBU'S GUARDS
A CAPTAIN
A BEAR
THE HORSE OF THE PHYNANCES
THE BRAIN EXTRACTOR
THE CREW
THE SHIP'S CAPTAIN

ACT I

◆ SCENE I ◆

Père UBU, Mère UBU

Père UBU

Crrrap!

Mère UBU

Hah! Very pretty, Père Ubu, ye are a fine great scoundrel!

Père UBU

Why don't I smash you, Mère Ubu!

Mère UBU

It's not me, Père Ubu, it's someone else you should assassinate.

Père UBU

By the wick of my candle,* I don't understand.

Mère UBU

Come now, Père Ubu, are you content with your lot?

Père UBU

By the wick of my candle, crrrap, Madam, in faith yes, I am content. Consider my advantages: Captain of dragoons, most trusted officer of King Wenceslas, decorated with the order of the Red Eagle of Poland, and former King of Aragon. What more do you want?

Mère UBU

What! Having been King of Aragon you're happy to march to

55

the parade-ground at the head of fifty fellows carrying pig-stickers when you could be setting the crown of Poland where once the crown of Aragon sat, on your noddle?

Père UBU

Hey, Mère Ubu, I can't understand a word you're saying.

Mère UBU

You're so stupid!

Père UBU

By the wick of my candle, King Wenceslas lives, a prosperous gentleman;* and supposing he should die, does he not have troops of children?

Mère UBU

What's stopping you from massacring the whole family and crowning yourself in their place?

Père UBU

Ah! Mère Ubu, you do me wrong and soon you'll be for the cooking pot.

Mère UBU

Hey, you poor fool, if I'm for the cooking pot, who'll mend the seat of your pants?

Père UBU

Well, and so what? Don't I have an arse like anyone else?

Mère UBU

In your place, that arse of yours, I'd want to put it on a throne. You could increase your riches endlessly, you could eat sausages regularly and roll round the streets in a carriage.

Père UBU

If I were king, I'd have them build me a monster head-dress like the one I had in Aragon which those Spanish scoundrels impudently stole from me.

Mère UBU

You could also procure yourself an umbrella and a greatcoat right down to your ankles.

Père UBU

Ah! I'm giving way to temptation. Bugger and crrrap, crrrap and bugger, if ever I meet him deep in the woods, he won't enjoy the experience.

Mère UBU

Just so. Père Ubu, now you are a real man.

Père UBU

But stay! Should I, a captain of dragoons, massacre the King of Poland! rather die!

Mère UBU,
aside

Oh! crrrap! (*To Père Ubu*) So, you plan to stay poor as a church mouse, Père Ubu?

Père UBU

God's guts! By the wick of my candle, I'd rather be poor as a skinny but decent church mouse than rich as a nasty fat cat.

Mère UBU

And the head-dress? And the umbrella? And the greatcoat?

Père UBU

Well, what about them, Mère Ubu?

He goes out, slamming the door

Mère UBU,
alone

Blast and crrrap, he was hard to shift, but blast and crrrap, I believe I've shaken him. God and myself willing, in eight days I could be Queen of Poland.

⚓ SCENE II ⚓

The scene is a room in Père Ubu's house and a magnificent spread is laid out on a table

Père UBU, Mère UBU

Mère UBU

Well! Our guests are very late.

Père UBU

Yes, by the wick of my candle! I'm bursting with hunger. Mère Ubu, you look really ugly today. Is it because we're expecting visitors?

Mère UBU,
shrugging her shoulders

Crrrap!

Père UBU,
grabbing a roast chicken

I say, I'm hungry. I'm going to bite this bird. It's a chicken, I believe. It's not too bad.

Mère UBU

What are you doing, you miserable wretch? What will our guests eat?

Père UBU

There's plenty left for them. I won't touch anything more. Mère Ubu, go to the window and see if our guests are arriving.

Mère UBU,
going there

I can't see anything.

During this time, Père UBU *pinches a round of veal*

Mère UBU

Ah! Here's Captain Brubbish arriving with his partisans. What are you eating, Père Ubu?

Père UBU

Nothing, just a bit of veal.

Mère UBU

Oh God! The veal! The veal! Veal! He's eaten the veal! Help!

Père UBU

By the wick of my candle, I'll tear out your eyes.
The door opens

♒ *SCENE III* ♒

Père UBU, Mère UBU, CAPTAIN BRUBBISH and his
PARTISANS

Mère UBU

Good day, gentlemen, we were eagerly awaiting you. Pray be
seated.

CAPTAIN BRUBBISH

Good day, Madam. But where is Père Ubu?

Père UBU

Here I am! Gadzooks, by the wick of my candle, I'm surely fat
enough.

CAPTAIN BRUBBISH

Good day, Père Ubu. Sit down, men.

They all sit down

Père UBU

Phew! a bit more, and I'd have gone through my chair-
seat.

CAPTAIN BRUBBISH

Well, Mère Ubu! What delicious food have you prepared for us
today?

Mère UBU

Here's the menu.

Père UBU

Ah! That's something interesting.

Mère UBU

Polish soup, ratlet cutlets, veal, chicken, dog pâté, parson's nose of turkey, charlotte russe...

Père UBU

Eh! that's enough, I should think. Is there any more?

Mère UBU,
continuing

Bombe glacée, salad, fruit, dessert, gruel, fartichokes, cauliflower à la crrrap.

Père UBU

Hey! Do you take me for the Emperor of the Orient that you spend so much money?

Mère UBU

Don't listen to him. He's a half-wit.

Père UBU

Ha! I'm going to sharpen my teeth on your calves.

Mère UBU

Eat up instead, Père Ubu. Here's your Polish soup.

Père UBU

Bugger me, how nasty it is.

CAPTAIN BRUBBISH

It's not nice, I agree.

Mère UBU

You bunch of creeps, what more d'you want?

Père UBU,

tapping his forehead

Oh! I've had an idea! I'll come back right away.

Exit UBU

Mère UBU

Gentlemen, let us taste the veal.

CAPTAIN BRUBBISH

It was delicious, I've finished.

Mère UBU

Now for the parson's noses.

CAPTAIN BRUBBISH

Exquisite, Exquisite! Up with Mère Ubu.

ALL

Up with Mère Ubu.

Père UBU,

entering

And you will soon be shouting up with Père Ubu.

He is holding an unspeakable lavatory brush and he throws it onto the banqueting table

Mère UBU

You miserable wretch, what are you doing?

Père UBU

Go on, taste that.

Several people taste it and fall down poisoned

Père UBU

Mère Ubu, pass me the ratlet cutlets, and let me dish them out.

Mère UBU

Here they are.

Père UBU

Get out all of you! Captain Brubbish, I've something to say to you.

THE OTHERS

Hey! we haven't finished eating.

Père UBU

What do you mean, you haven't finished eating! Get out, everybody! Brubbish, stay behind.

Nobody moves

Père UBU

Haven't you gone yet? By the wick of my candle, I'll knock you out with the ratlet cutlets.

He starts throwing them about

EVERYBODY

Ow! Ouch! Help! Save yourselves! Horrors! I'm dying!

Père UBU

Crrrap, crrrap, crrrap. Get out! I know what I'm doing!

EVERYBODY

Each man for himself! You wretch, Père Ubu! Traitor and down-and-out ruffian!

Père UBU

Ah, now they've gone. I can breathe again, but I've had a lousy dinner. Come, Brubbish.

Exeunt with Mère UBU

⚜ *SCENE IV* ⚜

Père UBU, Mère UBU, CAPTAIN BRUBBISH

Père UBU

Well, Captain, did you have a good dinner?

CAPTAIN BRUBBISH

Excellent, Sir, except for the crrrap.

Père UBU

What! the crrrap wasn't bad.

Mère UBU

Each man to his taste.

Père UBU

Captain Brubbish, I've decided to make you Duke of Lithuania.

CAPTAIN BRUBBISH

What! I thought you were down and out, Père Ubu.

Père UBU

In a few days, if you'll help me, I shall rule Poland.

CAPTAIN BRUBBISH

Are you going to kill Wenceslas?

Père UBU

The bugger's not stupid, he's guessed.

CAPTAIN BRUBBISH

If it's a matter of killing Wenceslas, you can count on me.
I'm his deadly enemy and I can answer for my men.

Père UBU,
rushing to kiss him

Oh! Oh! I love you dearly, Brubbish.

CAPTAIN BRUBBISH

Pooh! You stink, Père Ubu. Don't you ever wash?

Père UBU

Scarcely ever.

Mère UBU

Never!

Père UBU

I'm going to stamp on your feet.

Mère UBU

Big fat crrrap!

Père UBU

You may go, Brubbish, I've finished with you. But by the wick of my candle, I swear by Mère Ubu to make you Duke of Lithuania.

Mère UBU

But...

Père UBU

Be silent, sweet child...

Exeunt

⚊ SCENE V ⚊

Père UBU, Mère UBU, A MESSENGER

Père UBU

What do you want, Sir? Piss off. You tire me.

MESSENGER

Sir, you've been summoned by his Majesty the king.

Exit MESSENGER

Père UBU

Oh! Crrrap, buggeration, and by the wick of my candle, they've found me out, they'll chop off my head! Alas! Alas!

Mère UBU

What a ninny! And time is short.

Père UBU

Oh! I've had an idea: I'll say it was Mère Ubu and Brubbish.

66

Mère UBU

Hey! You big fat P.U., if you dare do that...

Père UBU

Well, I'm off to do it straight away.

Exit

Mère UBU,
running after him

Oh! Père Ubu, Père Ubu, I'll give you some sausages.

Exit

Père UBU,
in the wings

Oh! Crrrap! you're a silly sausage yourself!

⚊ *SCENE VI* ⚊

The King's Palace
KING WENCESLAS, *surrounded by his* OFFICERS;
BRUBBISH; THE KING'S SONS, BOLESLAS, LADISLAS, *and*
BUGGERLAS, *then* UBU

Père UBU,
entering

Oh! you know, it wasn't me, it was Mère Ubu and Brubbish.

67

THE KING

What ails you, Père Ubu?

BRUBBISH

He's had too much to drink.

THE KING

Just like me this morning.

Père UBU

Yes, I'm pissed because I've drunk too much French wine.

THE KING

Père Ubu, I desire to reward the many services you have rendered me in your capacity as captain of dragoons. This day I dub you Count of Sandomierz.*

Père UBU

Oh! my lord Wenceslas, I don't know how to thank you.

THE KING

Do not thank me, Père Ubu. Make sure you are at the grand parade tomorrow morning.

Père UBU

I'll be there. But do me the honour of accepting this tiny tin whistle.

He presents a tin whistle to the king

THE KING

What do you expect me to do with a tin whistle? I'll give it to Buggerlas.

YOUNG BUGGERLAS

What an ass Père Ubu is.

Père UBU

And now, I must piss off. (*As he turns away, he falls*) Ouch! Ow! Help! By the wick of my candle, I've exploded my intestines and punctured my paunch!

THE KING,
raising him up

Père Ubu, are you hurt?

Père UBU

Yea, verily, and I must surely kick the bucket. What will become of Mère Ubu?

THE KING

We will provide for her welfare.

Père UBU

You are graciously kind. (*Going out*) Yes, but, King Wenceslas, you're going to be massacred just the same.

≈≈ *SCENE VII* ≈≈

Ubu's House

GYRON, PILE, COTTISE, Père UBU, Mère UBU,
CONSPIRATORS and SOLDIERS, CAPTAIN BRUBBISH

Père UBU

Now, my fine friends, it's high time to work out the plans for our conspiracy. Let each man give his opinion. I'll give mine first, if you'll allow me.

CAPTAIN BRUBBISH

Speak, Père Ubu.

Père UBU

Well then, my friends, I suggest we simply poison the king by bunging some arsenic into his lunch. When he tries to guzzle it he'll fall down dead, and so I will be king.

EVERYBODY

Ugh, the smelly old tramp!

Père UBU

What, don't you like my plan? All right, then, let Brubbish give his opinion.

CAPTAIN BRUBBISH

My personal opinion is that we should whack him with our swords and unseam him from the nave to the chaps.*

EVERYBODY

Ay! That would be noble and valiant!

Père UBU

And what if he kicks you up the pants? I remember now—on parades, he wears iron shoes which hurt a lot. If I could, I'd sneak off to denounce you and get myself out of this mess. I believe he'd give me some cash as well.

Mère UBU

Oh! you traitor, you coward, you base and dull knave.

EVERYBODY

Down with Père Ubu! Spit on him!

Père UBU

Come now, Sirs, just keep quiet or I'll pop you in my pocket. Very well, I consent to expose myself to danger for your sakes. And so, Brubbish, it falls to you to run the king through.

CAPTAIN BRUBBISH

Wouldn't it be better to fling ourselves on him all together, bawling and bellowing? In this manner, we'd stand a chance of carrying the army with us.

Père UBU

Right. This is what we do. I'll try to stamp on his feet, he'll object, and then I'll say to him CRRRAP! That'll be the signal for you to fling yourselves upon him.

Mère UBU

Yes, and as soon as he's dead you must take his sceptre and his crown.

CAPTAIN BRUBBISH

And I and my men will chase after the royal family.

Père UBU

Yes, and I particularly commend young Buggerlas to you.

Exeunt

Père UBU,
running after them and bringing them back

Gentlemen, we have forgotten an essential part of the ceremony. We must swear to fight valiantly.

CAPTAIN BRUBBISH

But how can we? We have no priest.

Père UBU

Mère Ubu will take the place of a priest.

EVERYBODY

Let it be so.

Père UBU

And so, you swear to kill the king good and proper?

EVERYBODY

We swear it. Up with Père Ubu!

END OF ACT I

ACT II

⚅ SCENE I ⚅

The King's Palace
WENCESLAS, QUEEN ROSEMONDE, BOLESLAS,
LADISLAS, and BUGGERLAS

THE KING

Sirrah Buggerlas, this morning you insulted my Lord Ubu,
Knight of my Order and Count of Sandomierz. For this reason
I forbid you to appear at my parade.

THE QUEEN

Nevertheless, Wenceslas, you need your whole family to protect you.

THE KING

Madam, I never go back on my word. Your idle prattle tires me.

YOUNG BUGGERLAS

I submit, noble father.

THE QUEEN

But, Sire, are you still determined to attend this parade?

THE KING

And why not, Madam?

THE QUEEN

Yet once again, did I not see him in a dream smite you with all
his weapons and throw you into the Vistula, and an eagle like
the one on the Polish coat of arms place a crown upon his head?

THE KING

Whose head?

THE QUEEN

Père Ubu's.

THE KING

What madness! My Lord of Ubu is a noble gentleman, who would let himself be hung, drawn, and quartered to serve me.

THE QUEEN and BUGGERLAS

How wrong you are.

THE KING

Silence, young rascal. As for you, Madam, to prove how little I fear my Lord Ubu, I intend to go to the parade just as I am, with no arms and no sword.

THE QUEEN

O fatal rashness! I shall never look on you alive again.

THE KING

Come, Ladislas, come Boleslas.

Exeunt. THE QUEEN *and* BUGGERLAS *go to the window*

THE QUEEN and BUGGERLAS

May God and holy Saint Nicholas keep you.

THE QUEEN

Buggerlas, come to the chapel to pray for your father and your brothers.

74

⚌ *SCENE II* ⚌

The Parade Ground

THE POLISH ARMY, THE KING, BOLESLAS, LADISLAS,
Père UBU, CAPTAIN BRUBBISH and his MEN, GYRON,
PILE, COTTISE

THE KING

Noble Père Ubu, attend me with your followers for the inspection of the troops.

Père UBU,
to his followers

Watch it, you lot. (*To the king*) We're coming, Sire, We're coming.

UBU'S MEN *surround the king*

THE KING

Ah! Here is the regiment of the Danzig horse guards. They look very fine, i'faith.

Père UBU

Do you think so? They look pathetic to me. Look at this one. (*To the soldier*) How long is it since you cleaned yourself up, you ignoble creep?

THE KING

But this soldier is perfectly turned out. What's wrong with you, Père Ubu?

Père UBU

This!

He crushes his foot

THE KING

Miserable wretch!

Père UBU

Crrrap! Come on, men!

BRUBBISH

Hurrah! Forward!

They all smite the king, A PILLODIN *explodes*

THE KING

Help! Holy Virgin, I am dead.

BOLESLAS,
to Ladislas

What's all this? Draw your sword.

Père UBU

Aha! I've got the crown! Now for the others.

CAPTAIN BRUBBISH

Let's get the traitors!!

THE KING'S SONS *flee, everybody chases them*

≈ *SCENE III* ≈

THE QUEEN and BUGGERLAS

THE QUEEN

At last I feel more reassured.

BUGGERLAS

You've nothing to fear.

A fearful din is heard outside

BUGGERLAS

Ah! What do I see? My two brothers pursued by Père Ubu and his men.

THE QUEEN

Oh! my God! Holy Virgin, they are losing, they are losing ground!

BUGGERLAS

The whole army's following Père Ubu. There's no sign of the king. O fearful sight! Help us!

THE QUEEN

See, Boleslas dies! A bullet has got him.

BUGGERLAS

Hey! Ladislas! (LADISLAS *turns round*) Defend yourself! Hurrah for Ladislas!

THE QUEEN

Oh! They've surrounded him.

77

BUGGERLAS

He's done for. Brubbish has just cut him in two like a sausage.

THE QUEEN

Alas! Alas! These madmen are inside the palace, they're coming up the stairs.

The din increases

THE QUEEN and BUGGERLAS,
on their knees

My God, protect us.

BUGGERLAS

Oh! That Père Ubu! That wretch, that scoundrel, if I could get hold of him...

⚍ *SCENE IV* ⚍

THE SAME

The door is broken down. Enter Père UBU *and his frantic men*

Père UBU

Well, Buggerlas, what would you do with me?

BUGGERLAS

Praise be to God! I'll protect my mother even unto death! The first man to come forward dies.

Père UBU

O dear! Brubbish, I'm scared! Please let me go away.

A SOLDIER

comes forward

Yield, Buggerlas!

YOUNG BUGGERLAS

Take that, you knave! This is for you!

He splits his skull

THE QUEEN

Hold firm, Buggerlas, hold firm!

SEVERAL MEN,

coming forward

Buggerlas, we promise to spare your life.

BUGGERLAS

You scoundrels, you boozers, you scum!

He whirls round with his sword and massacres them

Père UBU

Huh! I'll deal with him just the same!

BUGGERLAS

Mother, fly by the secret stair.

THE QUEEN

But what of you, my son, what of you?

BUGGERLAS

I'll follow you.

Père UBU

Try to catch the Queen. Oh! She's gone. As for you, you wretch!...

He moves towards Buggerlas

BUGGERLAS

Aha! Glory be to God! This is my revenge!

*With a terrible blow of his sword, he splits his belly**

Mother, I follow you!

He disappears down the secret stairs

⚅ SCENE V ⚅

A cavern in the mountains

Enter YOUNG BUGGERLAS *followed by* ROSEMONDE

BUGGERLAS

We'll be safe here.

THE QUEEN

I doubt it not! Buggerlas, hold me up!

She falls on the snow

BUGGERLAS

Oh, mother, what ails you?

THE QUEEN

Believe me, I am sick, Buggerlas. I have but two more hours to live.

BUGGERLAS

What! Can it be the cold has struck you down?

THE QUEEN

How can I resist such bitter blows? The King massacred, our family destroyed, and you, scion of the noblest race that ever girt a sword, forced to flee to the mountains like an outlaw.

BUGGERLAS

And who forced me, dear God! Who? That vulgar Père Ubu, that adventurer, sprung up from heaven knows where, that loathsome creep, that base tramp! And when I think that my father decorated him and dubbed him count, and that on the morrow that base-born rogue did not scruple to lay hands on him!

THE QUEEN

O Buggerlas! When I recall how happy we were before the coming of that Père Ubu! But now, alas! Everything is changed!

BUGGERLAS

What can I say! Let us wait in hope and never give up our rights.

THE QUEEN

'Tis my hope for you, dear son, but for my part, I shall not live to see that happy day.

BUGGERLAS

Why, what ails you? She turns pale, she falls, help! But I am in the wilderness! Oh, my God! Her heart has ceased to beat. She is dead! Can this be? Yet another victim of Père Ubu! (*He hides his face in his hands and weeps*) How sad to be alone in the world, only fourteen years old, and with a terrible wrong to avenge!

He falls prey to the most violent despair

Meanwhile, THE SOULS OF WENCESLAS, *of* BOLESLAS, *of* LADISLAS, *and of* ROSEMONDE *come into the cave,* THEIR ANCESTORS *accompany them and fill the cave. The oldest approaches Buggerlas and gently rouses him*

BUGGERLAS

Why, what do I see? my whole family, my ancestors... What means this miracle?

THE SPECTRE

Learn, O Buggerlas, that whilst I lived I was Lord Mathias of Königsberg, the first king and the founder of our house. To you must fall the burden of revenge. (*He hands him a great sword*) And may this sword which I here give to you never rest till it has struck death to the usurper.

All disappear and BUGGERLAS *remains alone in a rapt attitude*

82

⚜ *SCENE VI* ⚜

The King's Palace
Père UBU, Mère UBU, CAPTAIN BRUBBISH

Père UBU

No, I won't, not me! Do you want to ruin me for those nincompoops?

CAPTAIN BRUBBISH

But look, Père Ubu, can't you see the populace expect gifts in honour of this joyous accession?

Mère UBU

If you don't see to the distribution of meat and gold, you'll be overthrown within two hours.

Père UBU

Meat, yes! Gold, no! Send three old nags to the knackers, that's good enough for these ruffians.

Mère UBU

Ruffian yourself! Why was I landed with a brute like you?

Père UBU

I tell you once more, I want to get rich quick, I won't give them a penny.

Mère UBU

But all the treasures of Poland are in your hands.

CAPTAIN BRUBBISH

Yes, I happen to know that there's an enormous treasure in the chapel. We'll hand it out.

Père UBU

Don't you dare do that, you wretch!

CAPTAIN BRUBBISH

But, Père Ubu, if you don't make a hand-out, the populace won't pay their taxes.

Père UBU

Is that really true?

Mère UBU

Yes, Yes!

Père UBU

Oh, all right, I agree to everything. Get together three million. Roast a hundred and fifty oxen and sheep. I'll have some too, so it won't be so bad!

Exeunt

≛ *SCENE VII* ≛

The Palace courtyard full of populace
Père UBU crowned, Mère UBU, CAPTAIN BRUBBISH,
FLUNKEYS bearing meat

THE POPULACE

Here's the king! Long live the king! Hurrah!

84

Père UBU,
throwing gold

Here, that's for you. It wasn't any fun having to give you money, but you know, Mère Ubu insisted. At least promise me that you'll pay your taxes good and proper.

EVERYBODY

Yes, Yes!

CAPTAIN BRUBBISH

See, Mère Ubu, they're fighting over the gold. What a battle!

Mère UBU

It's truly horrible. Ugh! Look! one of them's had his head bashed in.

Père UBU

What a lovely sight! Bring more chests of gold.

CAPTAIN BRUBBISH

Supposing we arrange a race?

Père UBU

Yes, why not? (*To the populace*) My friends, you see this chest of gold, it contains three hundred thousand golden rose nobles, genuine sterling Polish currency. Those who wish to race, line up at the end of the courtyard. Set off when I wave my handkerchief. The winner gets the chest. As for the losers, their consolation prize will be this other chest which will be shared out between them.

EVERYBODY

Oh, yes! Long live Père Ubu! What a good king! Things weren't like this in the days of King Wenceslas.

Père UBU,

to Mère UBU, *joyously*

Listen to them!

All the populace line up at the end of the courtyard

Père UBU

One, two, three! Are you ready?

EVERYBODY

Yes! Yes!

Père UBU

Go!

They set off, knocking each other over. Yells and chaos

CAPTAIN BRUBBISH

They're coming! They're coming!

Père UBU

The one in front is losing ground.

Mère UBU

No, he's winning now.

CAPTAIN BRUBBISH

Oh! he's losing, he's losing! It's all over. The other's won!

The one who was second has won

EVERYBODY

Long live Michael Federovitch! Long live Michael Federovitch!

86

MICHAEL FEDEROVITCH

Sire, I hardly know how to thank Your Majesty...

Père UBU

Oh, my dear friend, it's a mere nothing. Take your chest back home, Michael; and you lot, share out the other one, take a coin each until there's nothing left.

EVERYBODY

Long live Michael Federovitch! Long live Père Ubu!

Père UBU

And you, dear friends, come and dine with me! Tonight the palace doors are open to all, come and be my guests at dinner!

THE POPULACE

Let's go in! Let's go in! Long live Père Ubu! He's the noblest of sovereigns!

They enter the palace. The noise of the orgy which lasts till morning is heard. Curtain

END OF ACT II

ACT III

▬ SCENE I ▬

The Palace
Père UBU, Mère UBU

Père UBU

By the wick of my candle, here I am, king of this country. I've gorged so much I've got indigestion and they're just going to bring me my monster head-dress.

Mère UBU

What's it made of, Père Ubu? Although we're kings, we must be economical, you know.

Père UBU

Madam my she-woman, it's made of sheepskin with a clasp and tapes made of dogskin.

Mère UBU

That sounds lovely, but being king and queen is lovelier still.

Père UBU

Yes, you were right, Mère Ubu.

Mère UBU

We owe a debt of gratitude to the Duke of Lithuania.

Père UBU

Who?

Mère UBU

Why, Captain Brubbish.

88

Père UBU

I do beseech you, Mère Ubu, speak to me no more of that nincompoop. Now that I no longer need him, he can crawl on his belly, but he won't get his duchy.

Mère UBU

You do him great wrong, Père Ubu, he'll turn against you.

Père UBU

What, that pathetic little man? He worries me no more than Buggerlas.

Mère UBU

So you think you've seen the last of Buggerlas?

Père UBU

By my finance-sabre, of course I do! What d'you think he could do to me, that fourteen-year-old creep?

Mère UBU

Père Ubu, hearken to my words. Believe me, seek to win over Buggerlas by your kindness.

Père UBU

What, give away more money? Oh no, on no account! you've made me waste a good twenty-two million.

Mère UBU

Have it your own way, Père Ubu, but you'll stew for it.

Père UBU

Well, then, you'll be with me in the stew-pot.

89

Mère UBU

Once more, hear me! I'm sure that young Buggerlas will carry the day, for he has right on his side.

Père UBU

What filthy nonsense. Isn't wrong as good as right? Ah! you insult me, Mère Ubu, I'm going to cut you in pieces.

Exit Mère UBU *pursued by* UBU

▬ *SCENE II* ▬

The great hall in the Palace
Père UBU, Mère UBU, OFFICERS and SOLDIERS; GYRON,
PILE, COTTISE, NOBLES in chains, FINANCIERS,
MAGISTRATES, CLERKS

Père UBU

Fetch the Nobles' chest and the Nobles' hook, the Nobles' knife and the Nobles' book! Then bring in the Nobles.

THE NOBLES *are brutally pushed forward*

Mère UBU

I beseech you, be reasonable, Père Ubu.

Père UBU

I have the honour of telling you that to enrich the kingdom I shall put all the Nobles to death and confiscate their goods.

NOBLES

Oh, horror! Help us, populace and soldiers!

Père UBU

Bring forward the first Noble and pass me the Nobles' hook. Those who are condemned to death, I will push them through the trapdoor, they'll fall into the dungeon of the pig-pincher and of the money-chamber, where their brains will be extracted. (*To the Noble*) Who are you, nincompoop?

THE NOBLE

I am the Count of Vitebsk.

Père UBU

How much are your revenues?

THE NOBLE

Three million silver dollars.

Père UBU

Condemned to death!

He grabs him with the hook and pushes him down the hole

Mère UBU

What brutal savagery!

Père UBU

Second Noble, who are you? (THE NOBLE *doesn't answer*) Will you answer me, nincompoop?

THE NOBLE

Grand Duke of Posen.

Père UBU

Excellent! Excellent! I could ask for nothing better. Through the trapdoor. Third Noble, who are you? You've an ugly mug.

THE NOBLE

Duke of Courland, of the cities of Riga, of Reval, and of Mitau.

Père UBU

Very good! Very good! Have you nothing else?

THE NOBLE

Nothing.

Père UBU

Through the trapdoor, in that case. Fourth Noble, who are you?

THE NOBLE

Prince of Podolia.

Père UBU

How big are your revenues?

THE NOBLE

I'm ruined.

Père UBU

Just for those unkind words, you can go through the trapdoor. Fifth Noble, who are you?

THE NOBLE

Margrave of Thorn, Palatine of Polotsk.

Père UBU

Pretty feeble. Have you no other else?

THE NOBLE

That was enough for me.

Père UBU

Oh well, it's better than nothing. Down the trapdoor. What are you woaling about, Mère Ubu?

Mère UBU

You're too savage, Père Ubu.

Père UBU

Well, I'm getting myself rich. Make them read MY list of MY possessions. Clerk, read me MY list of MY possessions.

CLERK

County of Sandomierz.

Père UBU

Begin with the principalities, you stupid bugger!

CLERK

Principality of Podolia, Grand-Duchy of Posen, Duchy of Courland, County of Sandomierz, County of Vitebsk, Palatinate of Polotsk, Margraviate of Thorn.

Père UBU

And what comes next?

CLERK

That's all.

Père UBU

What d'you mean, that's all! Oh well, then, come on forward, Nobles. Since I haven't finished getting rich, I'm going to have all the Nobles put to death, and then I'll take all their unclaimed wealth. Come on, push all the Nobles through the trapdoor.

THE NOBLES *are piled through the trapdoor*

Hurry up, faster, now I want to make some laws.

SEVERAL VOICES

We'll see about that.

Père UBU

First I'm going to reform the legal system, and after that we'll proceed to the finances.

SEVERAL MAGISTRATES

We are opposed to all change.

Père UBU

Crrrap. To start with, magistrates will no longer receive payment.

MAGISTRATES

What will we live on? We're poor men.

Père UBU

You'll have the fines you impose and the goods of the people condemned to death.

A MAGISTRATE

Horrible.

A SECOND MAGISTRATE

It's disgraceful.

A THIRD MAGISTRATE

It's a scandal.

A FOURTH MAGISTRATE

It's an indignity.

ALL THE MAGISTRATES

We refuse to pass judgement under such conditions.

Père UBU

Through the trapdoor with all magistrates.

They struggle in vain

Mère UBU

Hey, what're you doing, Père Ubu? Who'll pass judgement now?

Père UBU

I will, come to think of it. You'll see how well it'll work.

Mère UBU

That'll be a fine kettle of fish.

Père UBU

Just shut up, you nincompoopaloid. Now, gentlemen, let us proceed to the finances.

FINANCIERS

Nothing needs changing.

Père UBU

What d'you mean? Me, I want to change everything. First of all I want to keep half the taxes for myself.

FINANCIERS

How shameless.

Père UBU

Gentlemen, we will institute a ten per cent tax on property, another on commerce and industry, a third on marriages, and a fourth on deaths, each one of fifteen francs.

FIRST FINANCIER

But, Père Ubu, that's idiotic.

SECOND FINANCIER

It's absurd.

THIRD FINANCIER

There's no rhyme or reason to it.

Père UBU

You're making a mock of me! Through the trapdoor with the financiers!

THE FINANCIERS *are flung in*

Mère UBU

But look here, Père Ubu, what sort of a king are you? You're massacring everyone.

Père UBU

Oh, crrrap!

Mère UBU

No more justice, no more finance.

Père UBU

Fear nothing, sweet child, I myself will go from village to village collecting taxes.

⚓ *SCENE III* ⚓

A peasant house on the outskirts of Warsaw. Several
PEASANTS are gathered there

A PEASANT,
entering

Amazing news! The king's dead, the dukes as well, and young
Buggerlas has escaped with his mother to the mountains.
Furthermore, Père Ubu's seized the throne.

ANOTHER

I have more news. I come from Cracow, where I saw them
carrying away the bodies of more than three hundred nobles
and five hundred magistrates who've been murdered. They say
the taxes are going to double and Père Ubu will come to collect
them himself.

EVERYBODY

Dear God! What will become of us? Père Ubu's a fearful villain
and they say his family's abominable.

A PEASANT

But listen; doesn't it sound as if someone's knocking at the
door?

A VOICE,
outside

Codswallop! Open up in the name of my crrrap, in the name of
St John, St Peter, and St Nicholas! Open up, open up, by my
sabre of finance, by my finance-horn! I've come to collect the
taxes!

97

The door is bashed in, enter UBU *followed by a crowd of money-grabbers*

⚊ *SCENE IV* ⚊

Père UBU

Which of you's the oldest? (A PEASANT *comes forward*) What do they call you?

THE PEASANT

Stanislas Leczinsky.

Père UBU

Well then, hornybelly! Listen carefully, or these gentlemen will cut off your hearoles. Now will you listen to me?

STANISLAS

But your Excellency hasn't said anything yet.

Père UBU

What d'you mean, I've been speaking for an hour. D'you think I've come here to preach in the wilderness?

STANISLAS

Perish the thought.

Père UBU

I've come therefore to tell you, to command you, and to signify unto you that you must produce and exhibit forthwith your finances, otherwise you'll be massacred. Come now, gentlemen

98

of the slippery finances, convey hither the conveyance of the phynances.

The conveyance is brought in

STANISLAS

Sire, we're entered on the register as owing a hundred and fifty-two silver dollars; we paid them more than six weeks ago come St Matthew's Day.

Père UBU

That may well be, but I've changed the government and I've made the newspapers announce that all taxes must be paid twice over and those which may be specified later shall be paid thrice over. This method will quickly make my fortune, then I'll kill everybody and go away.

THE PEASANTS

My Lord Ubu, we beseech you, have pity on us, we're poor citizens.

Père UBU

I don't give a damn. Pay up.

THE PEASANTS

We can't, we've paid already.

Père UBU

Pay up! Or Oi'll pop you in my pocket and there'll be torture and severance of the neck and of the head! Hornybelly, I believe I am the King!

EVERYBODY

So that's how it is! To arms! Up with Buggerlas, by the grace of God King of Poland and of Lithuania!

Père UBU

Forward, gentlemen of the finances, do your duty.

A battle is engaged, the house is destroyed, and old STANISLAS *escapes alone across the plain.* UBU *stays behind to pick up the finances*

⚊ SCENE V ⚊

A prison cell in the fortress of Thorn
BRUBBISH, in chains, Père UBU

Père UBU

Ah! Citizen, you see how it is, you wanted me to pay you what I owed you, so you rebelled because I didn't want to, you joined a conspiracy and now you're locked up. By my finance-horn, it serves you right, and the tables have been so neatly turned that even you must find it to your taste.

BRUBBISH

Beware, Père Ubu. In the five days that you've been king, you've committed more murders than would be needed to damn all the saints in Paradise to perdition. The blood of the King and the Nobles cries out for vengeance and its cries will be heard.

Père UBU

Hey, my fine friend, you've the gift of the gab. I daresay that if you escaped there might be complications; but I don't believe the dungeons of Thorn ever released any of the honest fellows placed in their tender care. That's why I'm saying good-night and I suggest you sleep fit to bust your hearoles, even if the rats dance a fine saraband in here.

Exit. Enter FLUNKEYS *and bolt all the doors*

▰ SCENE VI ▰

The Palace in Moscow
THE EMPEROR ALEXIS and his COURT, BRUBBISH

TSAR ALEXIS

So you are the base adventurer who conspired to put to death our cousin Wenceslas?

BRUBBISH

Sire, forgive me, I was carried away against my better judgement by Père Ubu.

ALEXIS

Oh, what a dreadful lie! So now what do you want?

BRUBBISH

Père Ubu had me imprisoned under pretext of conspiracy, I suceeded in escaping and I've been galloping across the steppes for five days and five nights to come and beg for your gracious pardon.

ALEXIS

What do you bring me as a pledge of your submission?

BRUBBISH

My adventurer's sword and a detailed map of the town of Thorn.

ALEXIS

I'll take the sword, but by St George, burn that map, I've no wish to owe my victory to treachery.

BRUBBISH

One of the sons of Wenceslas, young Buggerlas, still lives. I will do all that is in my power to regain the throne for him.

ALEXIS

What was your rank in the Polish army?

BRUBBISH

I commanded the fifth regiment of Dragoons of Wilma and a company of mercenaries under the command of Père Ubu.

ALEXIS

It is well. I here appoint you sub-lieutenant in the tenth Cossack regiment, and mind you do not betray us. If you fight well, you will be rewarded.

BRUBBISH

I'm not lacking in courage, Sire.

ALEXIS

It is well. Disappear from my presence.

Exit

⚜ SCENE VII ⚜

Ubu's Council Chamber

Père UBU, Mère UBU, COUNCILLORS OF THE PHYNANCES

Père UBU

Gentlemen, the session is open, try to listen attentively and keep quiet. First, we'll give an account of the finances, then we'll discuss a little system I've invented to bring good weather and get rid of rain.

A COUNCILLOR

Very good, my Lord Ubu.

Mère UBU

What a dim-wit.

Père UBU

Madam of my crrrap, beware, for I will not suffer your stupidities. As I was saying, gentlemen, the finances are going reasonably. A considerable number of dogs in woollen stockings spill out onto the streets every morning and the guttersnipes are working wonders. On all sides one can see nothing but burntdown houses and people groaning under the weight of our phynances.

THE COUNCILLOR

What about the new taxes, my Lord Ubu, are they going well?

Mère UBU

Not at all. The tax on the marriages has brought in only eleven cents so far, even though Père Ubu is chasing people all over the place to force them to get married.

Père UBU

By my sabre of the finances, wallop of my cod, my financial Madam, I have hearoles to speak with and you have a mouth to listen with. (*Roars of laughter*) No, that's not it! You're making me get it wrong, and it's your fault I'm stupid! But, by Ubu's horn! (*Enter* A MESSENGER) Well now, what's wrong with this one? Go away, you lout, or I'll pocket you with severance of the neck and dislocation of the legs.

Mère UBU

Ah! you've chucked him out, but here's a letter.

Père UBU

Read it. I think I'm losing my wits or perhaps I just can't read. Hurry up, you nincompoopaloid, it must be from Brubbish.

Mère UBU

Precisely. He says that the Tsar received him very kindly, that he's going to invade your territories to restore Buggerlas, and that you're going to be killed.

Père UBU

Oh! Oh! I'm scared! I'm scared! Ah! I fear I'll die. Oh! poor wretch that I am! What will become of me, dear God? This nasty man's going to kill me. St Anthony and all the saints, protect me, I'll give you some phynance, I'll burn candles for you. Gracious God, what will become of me? (*He weeps and sobs*)

Mère UBU

There's only one course to take, Père Ubu.

Père UBU

What's that, my love?

Mère UBU

War!!

EVERYBODY

Praise be to God! That's truly noble!

Père UBU

Oh yes, and I'll get beaten up again.

FIRST COUNCILLOR

Let's hasten to organize the army.

SECOND COUNCILLOR

And prepare our provisions.

THIRD COUNCILLOR

Make ready the artillery and the fortresses.

FOURTH COUNCILLOR

And collect money for the troops.

Père UBU

Oh! no, certainly not! You dare, I'm going to kill you. I don't want to give money away. What an idea! I was being paid for making war, but now I have to make war at my own expense! No, by the wick of my candle, let's make war, since you're mad about war, but don't let's spend a single penny.

EVERYBODY

Up with war!

⚓ *SCENE VIII* ⚓

The camp outside Warsaw

SOLDIERS and PILLODINS

Up with Poland! Up with Père Ubu!

Père UBU

Ah! Mère Ubu, give me my breastplate and my little bit of stick. I'll soon be so weighed down that I just wouldn't be able to walk even if I was being chased.

Mère UBU

Ugh, what a coward.

Père UBU

Ah! Behold, the crrrap-sabre is fleeing and the finance-hook can't hold out!!! I'll never make an end of it! The Russians are advancing and they're going to kill me.

A SOLDIER

My lord Ubu, behold, the hearole-scissors are falling.

Père UBU

Oi wull kill you with the hook for the crrrap and the knife for carving faces.

Mère UBU

How fine he is with his helmet and his breastplate, he looks like a pumpkin in armour.

Père UBU

Ah! now I'll mount my horse. Gentlemen, bring forward the horse of the phynances.

Mère UBU

Père Ubu, your horse can no longer carry you, he's eaten nothing for five days and is nearly dead.

Père UBU

That's a good one! They make me pay twelve sous a day for this nag and it can't even carry me. By the horn of Ubu, are you teasing me or have you been stealing from me? (*Mère* UBU *blushes and lowers her eyes*) Very well, let them bring me another beast, but I will not go on foot, hornybelly!

An enormous horse is led in

Père UBU

Let me mount it. Oh! get it to sit down! I'm going to fall off. (*The horse sets off*) Ah! Stop my horse, in God's name, I'll fall off and get dead!!!

Mère UBU

He really is an idiot. Ah! He's got up again and now he's fallen to the ground.

Père UBU

By my horn of physics, I'm half dead! But it's all the same to me, I'm off to war and I'm going to kill everybody. Watch out if you don't march straight. Oi wull put you in my pocket with twisting of the nose and the teeth and extraction of the tongue.

Mère UBU

Good luck, Lord Ubu.

Père UBU

I forgot to say I'm making you regent in my absence. But I've kept my books of finances, so if you steal it will be the worse for

you. I'm leaving the Pillodin Gyron as your assistant. Farewell,
Mère Ubu.

Mère UBU

Farewell, Père Ubu. Kill the Tsar properly.

Père UBU

I certainly will. Twisting of the nose and the teeth, extraction of
the tongue, and poking of the little bit of stick up the hearoles.

THE ARMY *moves off to the sound of fanfares*

Mère UBU,
alone

Now that great clown has gone, I must set my affairs in order,
kill Buggerlas, and lay my hands on the treasure.

END OF ACT III

ACT IV

⚜ *SCENE I* ⚜

The Crypt of the ancient kings of Poland in
Warsaw Cathedral

Mère UBU

Where's the treasure? None of the paving-slabs sounds hollow.
I was careful to count thirteen stones going along the walls
starting from the tomb of Ladislas the Great, and I can't find a
thing. They must have been deceiving me. But wait: here the
stone sounds hollow. To work, Mère Ubu. Come on, break the
seal round this stone. It won't budge. I'll try this piece of the
crook of the finances, it can still do its work. There! There's the
gold, amongst the bones of kings.* In the sack with all of it! Oh!
What's that noise? Do living souls still dwell among these
vaults? No, it's nothing, I must make haste. I'll take it all. This
money will be better off in the light of day than among the
tombs of the ancient princes. I must replace the stone. What's
that? Still the same sound. This place fills me with a mysterious
dread. I'll take the rest of this gold another time, I'll come back
tomorrow.

A VOICE,
coming from the tomb of John Sigismond

Never, Mère Ubu!

Mère UBU *runs off in terror, carrying the stolen gold out through the
secret door*

109

◄◄ *SCENE II* ►►

The main square in Warsaw
BUGGERLAS and his PARTISANS, the POPULACE
and the SOLDIERS

BUGGERLAS

Forward, my friends! Up with Wenceslas and Poland! That old scoundrel Père Ubu has gone, nobody's left but the old witch, Mère Ubu, with her Pillodin. I offer myself up to march at your head and to restore my father's dynasty.

EVERYBODY

Up with Buggerlas!

BUGGERLAS

And we'll abolish all the taxes imposed by the horrendous Père Ub.

EVERYBODY

Hurrah! Forward! Let's run to the palace and murder the hag.

BUGGERLAS

Aha! Look, there's Mère Ubu coming out of the palace with her guards!

Mère UBU

What do you want, gentlemen? Oh! It's Buggerlas!

The crowd throws stones

FIRST GUARD

All the windows are broken.

SECOND GUARD

By St George, they've struck me down.

THIRD GUARD

Goddammit, I'm dying.

BUGGERLAS

Keep throwing stones, my friends.

PILLODIN GYRON

Aha! It's like that, is it?

He draws his sword and rushes at them, wreaking absolute havoc

BUGGERLAS

Have at you! On guard, you crackbrained coward!

They fight

GYRON

I'm dying.

BUGGERLAS

Victory, my friends! Now for Mère Ubu!

Trumpets are heard

BUGGERLAS

Ah! Here come the Nobles. Let's run and catch the evil old harpy!

EVERYBODY

And then we'll strangle the old ruffian!

Mère UBU escapes pursued by all the Poles. Pistol-shots and hails of stones

▬ SCENE III ▬

The Polish army on the march in the Ukraine

Père UBU

God's horn, God's knees, and cow's features! We're about to perish, for we're dying of thirst and feeling fatigued. Master Soldier, have the goodness to carry our helmet of the finances, and you, Master Lancer, take charge of the scissors of the crrrap and the baton of the physics to relieve our person, for, I repeat, we are fatigued.

THE SOLDIERS *obey*

PILE

Hey! My Loid! it's amazing the Russians haven't shown up.

Père UBU

It is regrettable that the state of our finances does not permit us to have a carriage to match our size; we feared we'd demolish our steed; so we've made the whole journey on foot, dragging our horse along by its bridle. But on our return to Poland, with the aid of our knowledge of physics and assisted by the enlightenment of our councillors, we'll invent a wind-powered carriage to transport the whole army.

COTTISE

See where Nicolas Rensky hastens towards us.

Père UBU

What's wrong with the boy?

RENSKY

All is lost. Sire, the Poles are in revolt. Gyron's been killed and Mère Ubu's fled to the mountains.

Père UBU

You creature of the night, you bird of ill-omen, you screech-owl in gaiters! Who told you such nonsense? Tell us another! Who did this deed? I bet it was Buggerlas. Whence have you come?

RENSKY

From Warsaw, noble lord.

Père UBU

You boy of my crrrap, if I believed you I'd make the whole army turn back. But, my lord boy, your shoulders sport more feathers than brains and you have dreamed of folly. Go forward to our outposts, my boy. The Russians are not far now and soon we'll be running them through with our arms of the crrrap and the phynances and the physics.

GENERAL LASKY

Père Ubu, do not you see the Russians yonder in the plain?

Père UBU

It's true, it's the Russians! I'm done for. If only I could go away, but no such luck, we're on a hill and we'll be the target of all their thrusts.

THE ARMY

Here come the Russians! Here comes the enemy!

Père UBU

Come, gentlemen, let us take up our positions for the battle. We ourselves will remain on the hill and will not be stupid enough to descend. I'll stand in the middle like a living citadel and the rest of you must circle round me. I command you to fill the guns with all the bullets they'll hold, for eight bullets are capable of killing eight Russians and that's eight of them off my back. We'll position the foot-soldiers at the bottom of the hill to encounter the Russians and kill them a bit, the cavalry behind them to fling themselves into the mêlée, and the artillery surrounding this windmill here to fire into the heap. As for ourselves, we'll remain inside the windmill and shoot through the window with the pistol of the finances, and we'll place the baton of the physics across the doorway, and if anyone tries to get in, beware the crook of the crrrap!!!

OFFICERS

Your orders will be obeyed, Sire.

Père UBU

So! Things are going very well, we will emerge victorious. What time is it o'clock?

GENERAL LASKY

Eleven in the morning.

Père UBU

Then let's dine, for the Russians will not attack before midday. My lord General, tell the soldiers to relieve themselves and to intone the Song of the Finances.

Exit LASKY

SOLDIERS and PILLODINS

Long live Père Ubu, our great financier! Ting-a-ling! Ting-a-ling! Ting-a-ling-a-ling!

Père UBU

O these good people, how I adore them! (*A Russian cannon-ball arrives and breaks one of the windmill's sails*) Ow! I'm scared, gracious God, I'm dead! and yet, no, I'm all right.

⚜ *SCENE IV* ⚜

THE SAME, A CAPTAIN then THE RUSSIAN ARMY

A CAPTAIN,
arriving

Sire, the Russians are attacking.

Père UBU

Well, so what, what can I do about it? It wasn't me who told them to. Nevertheless, gentlemen of the finances, let's make ready for battle.

GENERAL LASKY

A second cannon-ball!

Père UBU

Ah! I can't hold out. It's raining lead and iron and we might damage our precious person. Let us descend.

They all run down. The battle has been engaged. They disappear in clouds of smoke at the foot of the hill

A RUSSIAN,
smiting

In the name of God and of the Tsar!

RENSKY

Ah! I'm dead.

Père UBU

Forward! Hey, you, Sir, I'm going to catch you, 'cause you hurt me, do you hear? With your gun which won't go off, you boozy idiot!

THE RUSSIAN

Well, take that!

He fires a shot from his revolver

Père UBU

Ouch! I've been wounded, they've filled me full of lead, they've perforated me, I've had my last rites, I'm dead and buried. Well, but really! Aha! Got you! (*He tears him to pieces*) Take that! Now just you try to do that again!

GENERAL LASKY

Forward! Keep it up! Let's get beyond the ditch. Victory is ours!

Père UBU

Do you think so? Right now my brow is decorated with more lumps than laurels.

THE RUSSIAN CAVALRY

Hurrah! Make way for the Tsar!

Enter THE TSAR, *accompanied by* BRUBBISH *in disguise*

A POLE

Oh! Heaven help us! Each man for himself, here comes the Tsar!

ANOTHER

Oh! my God! he's got over the ditch.

ANOTHER

Wham! Bam! That dirty great bugger of a lieutenant has brained four of them.

BRUBBISH

Hey, you lot, you haven't finished your work! Here, John Sobiesky, this one's for you! (*He brains him*) Now for the others!

He massacres the Poles

Père UBU

Forward, friends. Grab that creep! Beat the Muscovites to pulp! Victory's ours. Up with the red eagle!

EVERYBODY

Forward! Hurrah! Gadzooks! Catch the dirty great bugger!

BRUBBISH

By St George, I'm done for.

Père UBU,
recognizing him

Aha! So it's you, Brubbish! Aha! my friend. We are well pleased; the whole company's well pleased to find you again. I'll have you simmered over a slow flame. Gentlemen of the finances, light the fire. Ouch! Ow! Ouch! I'm dead. I've been hit by a cannon-ball at the very least. Oh, my God, forgive me my sins! Yes, it is indeed a cannon-ball.

BRUBBISH

You've been shot by a pistol loaded with blanks.

Père UBU

Ha! You're making a mock of me! That's enough! Into my pocketses!

He flings himself on him and tears him to pieces

GENERAL LASKY

Père Ubu, we're pushing forward on all sides.

Père UBU

I can see that, but I can go no further, I've been riddled through with kicks up the pants, I want to sit down on the ground. Boo-hoo! my bottle!

GENERAL LASKY

Go and get the Tsar's bottle, Père Ubu.

Père UBU

Yes, I'll go right away. Come, then! Sabre of the crrrap, do your work, and you, crook of the finances, don't hold back. May the baton of the physics labour in a spirit of generous emulation and share with the little bit of stick the honour of massacring, gouging out, and exploiting the Muscovite Emperor. Forward, my Lord Horse of the Finances!

He flings himself on the Tsar

A RUSSIAN OFFICER

On guard, your Majesty!

Père UBU

Take that, you! Oh! Ouch! Ow! Well, really. Ouch! Sir, I'm sorry, please leave me alone. Ouch! Honestly, I didn't mean it!

He runs away, pursued by THE TSAR

Père UBU

Holy Virgin, this madman's pursuing me! What have I done, great God! Oh! goodness, I still have to get back over the ditch.

Oh! I can sense him behind me, and the ditch is ahead! Let's go for it and shut our eyes!

He jumps over the ditch. THE TSAR *falls in*

THE TSAR

Just brilliant! I've landed in it now!

THE POLES

Hurrah! the Tsar is down!

Père UBU

Oh! I scarcely dare turn round! He's fallen in. Aha! They're bashing him up and a good thing too. Come on, Poles, hit him as hard as you can, he's really tough, the wretch! Me, I don't dare look at him! And yet our prediction's come true, the baton of the physics has worked wonders and undoubtedly I'd have killed him utterly, were it not for the inexplicable terror which came to combat and annul all the strength of our courage. But then, incontinent, we turned our coat, and we owe our salvation to our prowess as a rider and the mighty hocks of our Horse of the Finances whose speed is equalled only by his strength and whose lightness of foot has contributed to his renown, as well as to the depth of the ditch which was conveniently situated beneath the feet of the enemy of ourselves, the self-same Master of the Phynances. This is a very fine speech, but no one's listening to me. What's this! Now it's all starting again!

THE RUSSIAN DRAGOONS *make a charge and deliver the Tsar*

GENERAL LASKY

This time, we've been routed.

Père UBU

Ah! Now's my chance to make myself scarce. Come now, my Lords the Poles, forward! or rather, retreat!

THE POLES

Each man for himself!

Père UBU

Come on! Get going. What a gang, what a stampede, what a crowd, how can I get myself out of this mess? (*He is jostled*) Hey, you, watch out, or you'll experience the sizzling valour of the Master of the Phynances. Ha! He's gone. Let's make a quick getaway while Lasky's not looking.

Exit. Then we see THE TSAR *and* THE RUSSIAN ARMY *passing in pursuit of the Poles*

⚜ SCENE V ⚜

A Cavern in Lithuania. It is snowing
Père UBU, PILE, COTTISE

Père UBU

Ah! What filthy weather, it's freezing hard enough to split a stone, and the person of the Master of the Finances is greatly inconvenienced.

PILE

Ahem! My Loid Ubu, have you recovered from your terror when you ran away?

Père UBU

Yes! I'm not scared any longer but I've still got the runs.

COTTISE,
aside

What a pig!

Père UBU

Hey, my Lord Cottise, how's your hearole?

COTTISE

My Loid, it's as well as it can be while still remaining very poorly. And the consequoince is, the lead is weighing me down and I haven't been able to get the bullet out.

Père UBU

Well, serve you right! That'll teach you to keep hitting other people. I demonstrated the noblest valour, and massacred four of the enemy with my own hand, but I didn't put my life in danger. And that's not counting all those who were already dead when we finished them off.

COTTISE

I say, Pile, do you know what became of young Rensky?

PILE

He got a bullet through his brain.

Père UBU

Just as the poppy and the dandelion in the flower of their youth are reaped by the pitiless reap of the pitiless reaper who pitilessly reaps their pitiful noddles,—even so young Rensky hath poppy-ed off. He fought well, 'tis true, but there were too many Russians.

PILE and COTTISE

Hey! My Loid!

AN ECHO

Heyrroi!

PILE

What's that? Let's arm ourselves with our bloides.

Père UBU

Oh! No! What cheek! I bet that's some more Russians! I've had enough! Well, it's no problem, Oi'll bung them in moi pocket.

⚍ *SCENE VI* ⚍

THE SAME

Enter a bear

COTTISE

Hey, My Loid of the Finances!

Père UBU

Oh, I say, look at that doggy-woggy. Isn't he sweet?

PILE

Watch out! Oh! what a gigantic bear; where've I put my cartridges?

Père UBU

A bear? Oh! what a horrible beast. Oh, wretched creature that I am, I'll be eaten up. May God protect me. And he's coming after me. No, it's Cottise he's after. Ah! I breathe again.

THE BEAR *flings himself on Cottise.* PILE *attacks it, slashing with his knife.* UBU *takes refuge on a rock*

COTTISE

Come to me, Pile! Come to me! Help, my Loid Ubu!

Père UBU

Nothing doing! Sort yourself out, my friend; at present, we're telling our rosary. It's not my turn to be eaten.

PILE

I've done, I've got him.

COTTISE

Hold hard, my friend, he's letting go.

Père UBU

Sanctificetur nomen tuum.*

COTTISE

You cowardly bugger!

PILE

Ah! he's biting me! Oh! dear God, help me, I die.

Père UBU

Fiat voluntas tua!

COTTISE

Ah! I've managed to wound him.

PILE

Hurrah, he's losing blood.

Amid the shouts of the Pillodins, THE BEAR *is bellowing with pain and* UBU *goes on mumbling*

COTTISE

Hold him tight, let me get at him with my exploding knuckleduster.

Père UBU

Panem nostrum quotidianum da nobis hodie.

PILE

Have you got him yet? I can't hold on any longer.

Père UBU

Sicut et nos dimittimus debitoribus nostris.

COTTISE

Ah! I've got him.

An explosion rings out and THE BEAR *falls dead*

PILE and COTTISE

Victory!

Père UBU

Sed libera nos a malo. Amen. Well, is he really dead? Can I
come down from my rock?

PILE,
contemptuously

Whenever you like.

Père UBU,
climbing down

You can flatter yourselves that if you're still alive to trample the
snows of Lithuania, you owe it to the magnanimous courage of
the Master of the Finances, who laboured, strove, and made

himself hoarse reciting paternosters for your salvation, who wielded the spiritual sword of prayer with as much courage as the skill you demonstrated wielding that temporal weapon, the exploding knuckleduster of the Pillodin Cottise here present. We elevated our devotion to the furthest limit, for we did not hesitate to climb the highest of rocks, that our prayers might reach Heaven more swiftly.

PILE

What a repellent ass!

Père UBU

It is indeed a fat brute. Thanks to me, you have food for supper. What a belly, gentlemen! The Greeks would have been more comfortable in there than inside the wooden horse,* and, my dear friends, for two pins we'd have been in there ourselves, verifying its inner dimensions with our own eyes.

PILE

I'm dying of hunger. What can we eat?

COTTISE

The bear!

Père UBU

Yes, but, my fine fellows, are you going to eat him raw? We haven't a way of lighting a fire.

PILE

Haven't we got our flints?

Père UBU

Yes, that's true. And also I believe I can see a little wood where there must be some dry branches. Go and fetch some, my Lord Cottise.

COTTISE *goes off through the snow*

PILE

And now, King Ubu, you must cut the bear up.

Père UBU

Oh no! He may not be dead. Now you, who've been half-eaten and bitten all over, you can do the job. I'll light the fire, while we wait for him to bring the wood.

PILE *starts to cut up the bear*

Père UBU

Oh! Watch out! It moved.

PILE

But, King Ubu, he's already icy cold.

Père UBU

What a shame, it would have been better to eat him hot. This will give indigestion to the Master of Finances.

PILE,
aside

How revolting. (*Aloud*) Help me a little, Monsieur Ubu, I can't do the whole job by myself.

Père UBU

No, I don't want to do anything, me! I'm tired, for sure!

COTTISE,
re-entering

What snow, my friends, you'd think we were in Castile or at the North Pole. Night is falling: in an hour it'll be dark. Let's make haste while we can still see.

Père UBU

Yes, do you hear, Pile? Hurry up. Hurry up, both of you! Put the brute on the spit, cook the brute! Me, I'm hungry!

PILE

Hey, that's just a bit too much! You get working or you won't have anything, d'you hear, you glutton?

Père UBU

Oh, it's all the same to me, I'm just as happy eating it raw, so sucks to you. And anyway, me, I'm sleepy!

COTTISE

What can we do, Pile? Let's cook the dinner on our own. He won't get any, that's all there is to it. Or perhaps we could give him the bones.

PILE

Very well. Ah, the fire's taken.

Père UBU

Oh! That's nice, it's cosy now. But I can see Russians everywhere. What a rout, dear God! Ah!

He falls asleep

COTTISE

I'd like to know if what Rensky said is really true, and Mère Ubu's really been dethroned. That wouldn't be impossible.

PILE

Let's finish making the supper.

COTTISE

No, we've more important matters to discuss. I believe it would be wise to ascertain the veracity of this news.

PILE

That's true, but should we abandon Père Ubu or stay with him?

COTTISE

Night brings counsel. Let us sleep; tomorrow we'll decide what must be done.

PILE

No, better take advantage of the darkness to disappear.

COTTISE

In that case, let's go.

They go

⚊ SCENE VII ⚊

UBU,

talking in his sleep

Aha! My Lord the Russian Dragoon, watch out, don't shoot in this direction, there are people here. Aha! Here's Brubbish, what a nasty beast, he looks like a bear. And Buggerlas is coming to attack me! The bear, the bear! Ah! See, he's fallen! How tough he is, my goodness! Me, I don't want to do a thing! Go away, Buggerlas! Do you hear, you rogue? Now here comes

Rensky, and the Tsar! Oh! they're going to beat me. And the Lady Rbue! Where did you get all that gold? You've taken my gold, you wretched woman, you've been poking around in my tomb which lies in Warsaw Cathedral, next to the moon. Me, I've been dead for ages, I was killed by Buggerlas, and buried in Warsaw, next to Vladislas the Great, and also in Cracow, next to John Sigismond, and also in Thorn in the cell, with Brubbish! Here he comes again. Get out, you cursed bear. You look like Brubbish. D'you hear me, you devilish brute? No, he can't hear, the guttersnipes have cut his hearoles off. Extract the brains, murrrder, chop off the hearoles, rip off the finances, and drink until you die, that's the life for the guttersnipes, that's the delight of the Master of the Finances.

He falls silent and sleeps

END OF ACT IV

ACT V

~~ *SCENE I* ~~

It is dark. Père UBU is sleeping. Enter Mère UBU who doesn't
see him. The stage is completely dark

Mère UBU

At last I'm safe. I'm alone here, which is just as well, but what a
frantic rush: I've crossed the whole of Poland in four days!
Every misfortune assailed me at once. No sooner had that fat
donkey gone, than I went down to the crypt to get rich. Shortly
after that I was almost stoned to death by that Buggerlas and his
angry men. I lost my knight, the Pillodin Gyron, who was so
enamoured of my charms that he fainted with pleasure when he
saw me, and even when he didn't see me, or so they say, which
is the quintessence of love. Poor boy, he'd have let himself be
cut in two for me. The proof of that is, he was cut in four by
Buggerlas. Bang, crash, smash! Oh, I thought I'd die. So then I
fled, pursued by the angry crowd. I left the palace, I arrived at
the Vistula, all the bridges were guarded. I swam across the
river, hoping by this means to wear out my persecutors. The
nobles gathered together and pursued me. I nearly perished a
thousand times, smothered beneath a pile of Poles all bent on
my ruin. At last I eluded their fury and after running through
the snow for four days away from what was once my kingdom,
I've come here to take refuge. I've neither eaten nor drunk for
four days. Buggerlas was pursuing me closely... Well, here I'm
safe. Ah! I'm dying of fatigue and cold. But I wonder what
happened to my big fat clown, I mean my most respectable
spouse? Boy, did I milk him of his money! Did I lead him by the

nose! And what about his Horse of the Finances who was dying of hunger, the poor creature didn't often see oats. That was a good one! But alas! I've lost my treasure! It's in Warsaw, and who can get at it now?

Père UBU,
beginning to wake

Grab Mère Ubu, chop off her hearoles!

Mère UBU

Oh! my God, where am I? I'm beginning to panic. Oh, no, good God!

> Thanks be to Heaven I have spied
> The sleeping Père Ubu, my Lord, right by my side.*

I'd better be sweet and nice. Well, now, my big fat husband, did you sleep well?

Père UBU

Very badly! That bear was tough! Battle of the voracious against the coriacious but the voracious have completely eaten and devoured the coriacious, as you will see when day dawns; d'you hear, my noble Pillodins?

Mère UBU

What's he babbling on about? He's even stupider than when he left. Who's he talking to?

Père UBU

Cottise, Pile, answer me, you sackful of crrrap! where are you? Oh! I'm scared. But someone's just been talking. Who was it talking? It wasn't the bear, was it? Crrrap! where are my matches? Oh! I lost them in the battle.

Mère UBU,
aside

I'd better take advantage of the situation and the darkness, and pretend to be a supernatural apparition and make him promise to forgive me my pilfering.

Père UBU

Hey! By St Anthony! someone's speaking. Oddsboddikins, hang me if they aren't!

Mère UBU,
in a cavernous voice

Yes, my Lord Ubu, someone is speaking indeed, and the trumpet of the archangel who will awaken the dead from the ashes and the dust at the end would speak no differently! Listen to this stern voice. It is the voice of St Gabriel, who gives nothing but good advice.

Père UBU

Oh yes, that's what they all say.

Mère UBU

Cease to interrupt, or I will be silent and your bellysack will be done for!

Père UBU

Ah! My paunchlet! I'll be quiet, and I won't say another word. Pray continue, Madam Apparition!

Mère UBU

As we were saying, my Lord Ubu, you're a big fat man!

Père UBU

Very fat, indeed, that's quite right.

Mère UBU

Silence, Goddammit!

Père UBU

Oh! angels don't swear!

Mère UBU,
aside

Crrrap! (*Continuing*) Are you married, my Lord Ubu?

Père UBU

Yes indeed, to an old bag who's the pits!

Mère UBU

I think you mean she's a charming lady.

Père UBU

She's a nightmare. She's all claws and talons, one just can't get hold of her.

Mère UBU

You must get hold of her through gentleness, my Lord Ubu, and if you get hold of her thus, you'll see that she's at least the equal of a Venus rich in delights.

Père UBU

What's that? Has somebody caught de lice?

Mère UBU

You're not listening, my Lord Ubu; lend us a more attentive ear. (*Aside*) I'd better hurry, it'll be daybreak soon. My lord Ubu, your wife is an adorable and delicious woman, without a single fault.

Père UBU

You're mistaken, there is not a single fault that she does not possess.

Mère UBU

Pray, silence! Your wife is not unfaithful to you.

Père UBU

I'd like to know who could possibly fancy her. She's a harpy!

Mère UBU

She doesn't drink!

Père UBU

Only since I took away the cellar key. Before that she was sloshed by seven o'clock in the morning and she perfumed herself with spirits. Now she perfumes herself with heliotrope and smells much the same. I don't care. But now I'm the only one who gets pissed!

Mère UBU

What a cretinous individual!—Your wife doesn't take your gold.

Père UBU

No, isn't it peculiar!

Mère UBU

She hasn't walked off with a single penny!

Père UBU

Witness my Lord, the noble and unfortunate Horse of the Phynances, who, not having been fed for three months, was obliged to conduct the whole campaign dragged along by his bridle through the Ukraine. And so the poor beast died in harness!

Mère UBU

You're telling lies, you've a model wife, and as for you, you're a monster!

Père UBU

I'm telling the truth. I've a hussy of a wife and as for you, you're a silly sausage!

Mère UBU

Beware, Père Ubu.

Père UBU

O, yes, it's true, I was forgetting who I was talking to. No, I never said that!

Mère UBU

You killed Wenceslas.

Père UBU

Well, naturally, it's not my fault, is it? Mère Ubu was the one who wanted it.

Mère UBU

You had Boleslas and Ladislas put to death.

Père UBU

Too bad for them! They wanted to bash me up!

Mère UBU

You failed to keep your promise to Brubbish and afterwards you killed him.

Père UBU

I'd rather it was me than him reigning in Lithuania. Right now it's neither the one nor the other. That proves it wasn't me that did it.

Mère UBU

There's only one thing you can do if you want your crimes to be pardoned.

Père UBU

What thing? I'm all ready to become a saintly man, I'd like to be a Bishop and have my name in the Church calendar.

Mère UBU

You must forgive Mère Ubu for having pinched a little money.

Père UBU

Well, I'll tell you what! I'll forgive her when she's given everything back, been thoroughly beaten, and resuscitated my Horse of the Finances.

Mère UBU

He's completely nuts about his horse! Oh, dear, I've had it, the day's dawning.

Père UBU

However, I'm glad to know for certain that my dear spouse was stealing from me. I know it now for sure. Omnis a Deo scientia,* which means: Omnis, all; a Deo, knowledge; scientia, comes from God. That's the explanation of the phenomenon. But Madam Apparition's got nothing more to say. I wish I could offer her some refreshment. What she was saying was extremely amusing. Aha, it's daylight! Oh, gracious God, by my Horse of the Finances, it's Mère Ubu!

Mère UBU,
cheekily

That's not true, I'm going to excommunicate you.

Père UBU

Aha! you slut!

Mère UBU

Such impiety.

Père UBU

Oh, you've gone too far. I can see that it's you, you stupid hussy! What the devil are you doing here?

Mère UBU

Gyron is dead, and the Poles have thrown me out.

Père UBU

And as for me, it's the Russians who threw me out: noble minds must meet.

Mère UBU

Or rather, one noble mind meets one donkey-brain!

Père UBU

Is that so? Well, now it's going to meet a palmiped.

He chucks the bear at her

Mère UBU,
falling crushed beneath the weight of the bear

Oh! Good God! Horrors! Ouch! I'm dying! I'm choking! He's biting! He's swallowing me! He's digesting me!

Père UBU

He's dead! you're grotesque. Oh, but come to think of it, perhaps he isn't dead, Oh, my God! No, he's not dead, I'd better escape. (*He climbs back onto his rock*) Pater noster qui es...

Mère UBU,
ridding herself of the bear

I say! Where's he got to?

Père UBU

Ah my God! Here she is again! The stupid creature, can't she be got rid of? Is the bear dead then?

Mère UBU

Well yes, you stupid ass, he's quite cold. How did he get here?

Père UBU,
embarrassed

I don't know. Oh, yes, I do! He was trying to eat Pile and Cottise and me, I killed him with a shot of paternoster.

Mère UBU

Pile, Cottise, paternoster, what's all that? He's mad, by my finance!

Père UBU

I'm telling you the precise truth! And you're an idiot, my fine bellysack!

Mère UBU

Tell me about your campaign, Père Ubu.

Père UBU

Oh! damn it all, no I won't, it would take too long. All I know is that in spite of my undeniable courage everybody beat me.

Mère UBU

What, even the Poles?

Père UBU

They were shouting 'Up with Buggerlas and Wenceslas!' I thought they were going to hang, draw, and quarter me. They were completely maddened! And then they killed Rensky!

Mère UBU

I couldn't care less! You know Buggerlas killed the Pillodin Gyron!

Père UBU

I couldn't care less! And then they killed poor Lasky!

Mère UBU

I couldn't care less!

Père UBU

Oh, now look here, just come over here, you slut! Down on your knees before your master. (*He grabs her and pushes her to her knees*) You're going to suffer your final punishment.

Mère UBU

Ouch, ouch! my Lord Ubu!

Père UBU

Ouch, ouch, ouch! what else, is that all? Me, I'm just beginning: twisting of the nose, tearing of the hair, poking of the little bit of stick up the hearoles, extraction of the brains through the heels, laceration of the posterior, partial or even total suppression of the marrow from the spine (if only it could make her character less spiny too), not forgetting opening out of the air-bladder and finally grand severance of the neck as originally seen in John the Baptist, the total being derived from the Holy Scriptures, both Old and New Testament, compiled, corrected, and perfected by the Master of the Finances all present and correct! Does that suit you, you silly sausage?

He begins to tear her to pieces

Mère UBU

Have mercy, my Lord Ubu!

Loud noise at the entrance of the cavern

⸺ SCENE II ⸺

THE SAME, BUGGERLAS,

rushing into the cavern with his soldiers

BUGGERLAS

Forward, my friends! Long live Poland!

Père UBU

Oh! Oh! hold on a minute, Mr Pole-Axe, hold on till I've finished with Madam my spouse!

BUGGERLAS,
hitting him

Take that, you coward! You varlet! You rascal! You scoundrel! You infidel!

Père UBU,
retaliating

Take that, you Polish turd, you drunkard, you bastard, you sluggard, you laggard, you dullard!

Mère UBU,
also hitting him

Take that, you capon, you glutton, you felon, you moron, you scullion, you carrion, you gorgon!

THE UBS RUSH UPON THE SOLDIERS *who defend themselves as best they can*

Père UBU

My God! What a lot of smashing!

Mère UBU

Watch our feet, my Polish gentlemen.

Père UBU

By the wick of my candle, will you pack it in, once and for all? Not another one! Ouch! If only I had my Horse of the Finances!

BUGGERLAS

Go on, hit them, keep on hitting them!

VOICES OFF

Up with Père Ubé, our great financier!

Père UBU

Ah! There they are. Hurrah! Here come the Pères Ubus. Come on, hurry up, we need you, gentlemen of the finances!

Enter THE PILLODINS, *who fling themselves into the fray*

COTTISE

Let's show the Poles the door!

PILE

Ha! We meet again, my Loid of the Finances. Forward, press them hard, make for the door, once we're outside it'll be easy to escape.

Père UBU

Oh, that's what I find easiest. Ouch! how hard he hits!

BUGGERLAS

My God! I've been wounded.

STANISLAS LECZINSKY

It's a mere scratch, Sire.

BUGGERLAS

That's right, I'm just a bit dazed.

JOHN SOBIESKY

Keep on hitting them, they're making for the door, the scoundrels.

COTTISE

We're getting there, everybody follow. As a resoilt of thois I can see dayloight.

PILE

Keep going, my lord Ubu!

Père UBU

Oh! I'm going all right, in my pants. Forward, by the horns of my haggis! On with the killing, bleeding, flaying, massacring, by the horn of Ubu! Ah! It's dying down!

COTTISE

There are only two of them left to guard the door.

Père UBU,

hitting them with the bear

That's done for this one, and that's done for that one! I'm outside! Let's escape! Follow me, men, and quickly!

☙ *SCENE III* ☙

The scene represents the province of Livonia covered with snow

THE UBS and their retinue, *in flight*

Père UBU

Ah! I think they've given up hope of catching us.

Mère UBU

Yes, Buggerlas has gone to be crowned.

Père UBU

I don't envy him his crown.

Mère UBU

You're quite right, Père Ubu.

They disappear into the distance

◆◆ *SCENE IV* ◆◆

The deck of a ship sailing close by on the Baltic. On the deck,
Père UBU and all his followers

THE CAPTAIN

Ah! What a delightful breeze.

Père UBU

The fact is, we're escaping with a prodigious rapidity. We must
be sailing at a million knots per hour at least, and the good thing
about these knots is that once they're done up they won't undo.
It's true that we have wind behind us.

PILE

What a pathetic imbecile.

A squall blows up, the ship lists and makes the sea foam

Père UBU

Oh! Ouch! Oh God! we're sinking. Your ship is going all
crooked, it's going to fall.

THE CAPTAIN

Everyman to leeward, haul the foresail!

Père UBU

Hey! For God's sake don't do that! Don't all go to the same side
of the ship! That's stupid, that is. Just suppose the wind changes
sides; everyone would go to the bottom and the fish would eat
us up.

THE CAPTAIN

Don't bear away, keep close to the wind!

Père UBU

No, no, do bear away. I'm in a hurry, I am! Bear me away, do you hear? It's your fault, you brute of a captain, if you don't bear us there, it's hard to bear. Aha! I'm in going to take charge myself now, in that case! Veer away! Bear to port! Bear to starboard. Drop anchor, go about! Veer the ship! Hoist the sails, strike the sails, tiller to starboard, tiller to port, tiller hard over! You see, it's all going very well. Keep broadside on to the sea and then everything will be perfect.

They all roar with laughter, then a stiff breeze blows up

THE CAPTAIN

Lower the main jib, full reef the topsails!

Père UBU

That's not bad, in fact it's quite good! Do you hear, gentlemen mariners? Lower the man's rib, pull free the entrails!

Several people are killing themselves laughing.
A wave hits the deck

Père UBU

Oh! What a deluge! This is the result of the manœuvres that we ordered.

Mère UBU and PILE

How delightful to mess about in boats!

A second wave hits the deck

PILE,
soaking wet

Watch out for the devil and his deep blue sea.

145

Père UBU

My Lord Boy, bring us something to drink.

They all settle down to drink

Mère UBU

Ah! How delightful that we should see once more the fair land of France, our old friends, and our castle of Mondragon!

Père UBU

Hum! we'll be there soon! We are at present passing beneath the castle of Elsinore.

PILE

My courage returns at the thought of seeing my beloved Spain.*

COTTISE

Yes, and we'll dazzle our compatriots with the story of our wonderful adventures.

Père UBU

Well, that goes without saying! Me, I'm going to get myself made Lord of the Finances in Paris.*

Mère UBU

Good idea! Ouch! What was that jolting?

COTTISE

It's nothing, we've just rounded the Cape of Elsinore.

PILE

And now our noble vessel is skimming rapidly over the dark waters of the North Sea.

Père UBU

That savage and inhospitable water which laps against the country known as Germany, thus named because the inhabitants of this country are all cousins german.

Mère UBU

That's what I call erudition. They say the country is most fair.

Père UBU

Ah! gentlemen! however fair, it can never match Poland. If there were no Poland, there would be no Poles!

THE END

BRAIN EXTRACTION SONG

(from *Ubu Cuckold*)

My job was as a carpenter
Out in the suburbs of Paree;
My wife worked as a dressmaker
We lacked for nothing, her and me.
On Sundays when the day was fine
We wore our smartest Sunday clothes
And went to have a lovely time
And watch the brain extraction show.
  See, see, the machines all turn,
  See, see, the brains all spurt,
  See, see, the rich men squirm;

Chorus: Yah, boo! Horny poo! Long live Père Ubu!

Our darling boys, all smeared with jam,
Each waved his little paper dolly
And sat with us aboard the tram
Which drove us there, all right and jolly.
The crowd squeezed up against the fence
We fought to get a front-seat view,
I had to climb up on a bench
To keep the bloodstains off my shoes.
  See, see, the machines all turn,
  See, see, the brains all spurt,
  See, see, the rich men squirm;

Chorus: Yah, boo! Horny poo! Long live Père Ubu!

Soon we were all white with brains;
The boys were thrilled, especially when
The big swords of the Pillodins

Would maim and kill and kill again.
Just then I saw by the machine
A bugger with an ugly stare.
'Hey, you,' says I, 'You look so mean.
You're for it now, and I don't care.'
   See, see, the machines all turn,
   See, see, the brains all spurt,
   See, see, the rich men squirm;

Chorus Yah, boo! Horny poo! Long live Père Ubu!

Just then my wife tugged at my sleeve.
Says she: 'This is your chance, you thug.
The Pillodin's not looking. Heave
A turd right at the rich man's mug.'
This clever plan convinced me quite.
I plucked up courage to begin,
And flung a hefty lump of shite
But missed, and hit the Pillodin.
   See, see, the machines all turn,
   See, see, the brains all spurt,
   See, see, the rich men squirm;

Chorus: Yah, boo! Horny poo! Long live Père Ubu!

Over the fence I had to roll,
The angry crowd manhandled me
And flung me head first down the hole,
The hole of no return, you see.
That's what you get when you're too keen
To see the brains spurt from the head,
To see the murdering machine,
You go out live, you come back dead.
   See, see, the machines all turn,
   See, see, the brains all spurt,
   See, see, the rich men squirm;

Chorus: Yah, boo! Horny poo! Long live Père Ubu!

THE MAMMARIES
OF TIRESIAS

by

Guillaume Apollinaire

PREFACE

Without begging your indulgence, I should like to point out that this is a youthful work, for apart from the Prologue and the last scene of Act II, added in 1916, the piece was written in 1903, in other words fourteen years before* it was performed.

I have called it a 'drama'—in the sense of 'action'—to stress just what it is that makes it different from those comedies of manners, comedy-dramas, and light comedies, which during the last half-century have provided the theatre with works which even when excellent are second-rate, and known to us simply as 'plays'.*

I have used a neologism to describe my drama, something I hardly ever do, so I hope I will be forgiven: I have created the adjective 'surrealist'.* It doesn't at all mean 'symbolic' as M. Victor Basch* assumes in his review article, but it quite accurately defines an artistic tendency which, while it may be no newer than anything under the sun, has at least never been used in the formulation of a creed, or a statement of artistic or literary faith.

The playwrights who succeeded Victor Hugo, in their commonplace idealism, sought verisimilitude in a clichéd local colour, which parallels the contrived naturalism of the comedy of manners, a form originating well before Scribe,* in the sentimental plays of Nivelle de la Chaussée.*

In attempting, if not to renew theatre, at least to make my personal contribution, I felt impelled to return to nature itself; though I did not imitate it as a photographer does.

When man resolved to imitate walking, he invented the

wheel, which does not look like a leg. In doing this, he was practising surrealism without knowing it.

I should add that I can't decide whether my drama is serious or not. It aims to be interesting and entertaining. That is the aim of all theatre. It also aims to give prominence to a vital question for everyone who understands the language in which it is written: the problem of repopulation.*

I could have taken this subject, which has never been treated before, and written a play along the sarcastic-melodramatic lines made fashionable by the writers of didactic plays.

I have preferred to adopt a less sombre tone, for I do not believe that theatre should bring despair to anyone.

Then, too, I could have written a play of ideas and pandered to the tastes of present-day audiences, who like to imagine themselves as thinkers.

Instead, I have chosen to give free rein to fantasy, my own way of interpreting nature, fantasy, which, from one day to the next, may appear more or less melancholic, satirical, or lyrical, but always, as far as possible, incorporates an element of common sense; although this element may be innovative enough to seem shocking or outrageous, it will nevertheless remain visible to people of good faith.

In my opinion, the subject is so moving that it even allows the word 'drama' to be given its most tragic sense; but if the French start having children again, the work could be called a farce from then on: it is up to them. Nothing could bring me greater patriotic pleasure. Believe me, the reputation which would be enjoyed by the author of the *Farce of Master Pierre Pathelin*,* if only we knew his name, keeps me awake at night.

I've been told that I have used some of the techniques of popular revues: I don't quite see where. Besides, this criticism can in no way harm me, for popular art is an excellent source, and I would have been proud to draw from it; but the fact is that all my scenes quite naturally follow my story-line, which tells of a man who produces children; this idea is new to theatre and indeed to literature in general, though it ought to seem no more shocking than some of the impossible inventions of novelists popular for their pseudo-scientific fantasies.

Furthermore, there are no symbols in my play, which is quite transparent; but people are free to see in it all the symbols they wish, and to tease out a thousand meanings, as though it were a Delphic oracle.*

M. Victor Basch, who has not understood, or perhaps has chosen not to understand, that the subject is repopulation, insists on seeing this work as symbolic; that is his prerogative. But he goes on: 'the first requirement of a symbolic play is that the relationship between the symbol, which is always a sign, and the thing signified, should be immediately discernible.'

This is, however, not invariably the case, for there are some remarkable works whose symbolism is actually open to many interpretations, which at times can seem contradictory.

I wrote my surrealist drama above all for the French, just as Aristophanes composed his comedies for the Athenians.

I warned them of the grave and widely recognized danger that threatens a nation, wishing to be prosperous and powerful, if its populace does not reproduce. I suggested that all they had to do to remedy the situation was to produce children.

M. Deffoux*, who is an amusing writer but seems to me to be a latter-day Malthusian, makes a ludicrous connection between the rubber[1] of the balloons and balls which represent the

---

[1] To clear myself of any ciriticism regarding the use of rubber breasts, herewith an extract from the newspapers proving that these items are strictly within the bounds of legality:

'Ban on Sales of Dummies, other than those of Pure Rubber, Vulcanized by Heat— On 28 February last, the *Journal Officiel* issued the law of 26 February 1917, amending

mammaries (this is perhaps where M. Basch finds his symbol), and certain items recommended by the Neo-Malthusians.* Frankly, they are completely irrelevant, for they are used far less in France than in any other country, whereas in Berlin, for instance, never a day goes by without one of them almost landing on your head as you walk through the streets, for the Germans use them a great deal, though they are a prolific race.

As well as the prevention of pregnancy by hygienic means, the other reasons given for depopulation, such as alcoholism, occur everywhere, to a much greater degree than in France.

In a recent study on alcohol, M. Yves Guyot comments that although France ranks first in the statistics on alcoholism, Italy, that famously sober country, comes second! This shows how little we can trust statistics; they play us false, we would be fools to trust them. Furthermore, it is surely remarkable that those provinces of France where the birth rate is highest are precisely those which come top in the statistics on alcoholism!

The fault is graver, the vice more deep-rooted, for the truth is this: the French no longer make children because they scarcely make love. That's all there is to it.

But I will dwell no longer on this subject. It would take a whole book, and a radical change in life-style is needed too. It's up to the people who govern us to take action, to make marriage

Article 1 of the law of 6 April 1910, which concerned only the banning of feeding-bottles with tubes.

Revised Article 1 of this law is henceforth formulated as follows:

It is forbidden to sell, offer for sale, display, or import:

1. Feeding-bottles with tubes;

2. Dummies and teats made of any product other than pure rubber, vulcanized by a process other than vulcanization by heat, and not displaying, with the maker's or retailer's stamp, the indication: "pure rubber".

Therefore only dummies and teats made of pure rubber and vulcanized by heat are allowed.' [*Author's note*]

an easier option, above all to encourage fertile love; other important aspects like child labour can easily be resolved later for the benefit and honour of our country.

To return to the art of the theatre, the essential qualities of the drama which I propose will be found in the Prologue to this work.

I should like my art of the theatre to be modern, simple, fast-moving, with such short-cuts or exaggerations as are necessary to make an impact on the audience. The subject should be general enough for the dramatic work based on it to influence people's ideas and behaviour, in the field of duty and honour.

Depending on the circumstances, tragedy will prevail over comedy, or vice versa. But I do not believe that from now on the public will patiently sit through plays unless they include these two opposing elements; for people nowadays, and the writings of our younger contemporaries, are filled with such energy that the greatest misfortune seems meaningful from the outset; we feel we can view it not only in a spirit of benevolent irony, which enables us to laugh at it, but also with genuine optimism, which immediately consoles us and gives us hope.

Besides, theatre is not life, any more than a wheel is a leg. Consequently, I feel it is legitimate to bring to the theatre new and striking aesthetic ideas, which enhance the visual impact and increase the theatricality of the staging, without altering the touching or comical aspect of dramatic situations, which should stand on their own merits.

Finally, I should add that in making my own way among contemporary literary movements, I am not claiming to be founding a movement; my principal aim is to protest against realism which is the dominant feature of modern dramatic art. Realism may well be appropriate for the cinema; but nothing is more alien to dramatic art.

I should add my belief that for the purposes of theatre the only appropriate spoken line is flexible, based on rhythm, subject-matter, and breathing patterns, which can be adapted to suit all theatrical requirements. A playwright should not reject the musical effect of rhyme. It should not take control, for modern writers and audiences will find this tedious; but it can add its own beauty to pathos or comedy, in choruses, sometimes in dialogue, at the end of certain soliloquies, or to close an act on a dignified note.

Does not such a dramatic art have infinite possibilities? It gives free rein to the imagination of the playwright, who, casting off all the bonds that had once seemed necessary, or, perhaps, renewing ties with a neglected tradition, does not see fit to reject the greatest of his predecessors. Here he pays them the tribute that we owe to those who have raised humanity above the lowly imaginings with which, left to its own devices and denied the help of men of genius able to rise above it and lead it onwards, it would have had to make do. But these men bring before our gaze new worlds to broaden our horizons, ever showing us more, and bringing us the joy and honour of ever advancing towards the most surprising discoveries.

TO LOUISE MARION[*]

Louise Marion you were a great sensation
Inflating all those tits with wit that's new

My tale has been a fruitful inspiration
Women have stopped aborting thanks to you
Now at your voice new life for France will dawn
In women's trembling bellies hope is born

TO MARCEL HERRAND

You played the man sublime ingenious
You brought forth children made new gods for us
Wiser more warlike loving more docile
Stronger than we were braver more allied
Victory sees their fortune with a smile
And celebrates with due prosperity
Your civic sense and your fecundity
One day they'll all become our City's pride

TO YETA DAESSLÉ

Were you really in Zanzibar Monsieur Lacouf
Did you die and die twice without even an ouf

Kiosk that moves bearer of news
You were the brains of the audience whose
Own brains sadly failed to perceive that they must
Have children or else they must all come to dust

You twice played the press which daily presents
To Europe as well as America sense
Already they echo those echoes of yours

Dear Daesslé my thanks
Now the endless small fry
Who proliferated through Act II of my play
Will be good little French girls and boys thanks to you
Pink and white just like you dear Madame they will stay
And we will have brought off a fabulous coup

TO JULIETTE NORVILLE

Now is the time Madame to hear the men at arms
I'm one of them that's why though it may cause alarms
I've spoken
Seated on your steed you were triumphal
You represented law and order as its symbol
We acted in the hope that France awakes and sees
How people must give birth if they're to dwell at ease
Just like the children of the husband of Therese

TO HOWARD

You played the people and remained mumchance

People of Zanzibar or rather men of France
You must abandon taste for reason's sway
Though loving home must travel far away
Must cherish daring seek adventure
Must always strive for France's future
Chance all your wealth and never rest expect
Learn what is new these facts you must perfect
When prophets cry their message don't neglect
And make more children that's what I recount
A child spells riches nothing else will count

CHARACTERS

THE DIRECTOR

THERESE/TIRESIAS

THE HUSBAND

THE POLICEMAN

PRESTO

LACOUF

THE KIOSK

THE PEOPLE OF ZANZIBAR

THE JOURNALIST

THE SON

A LADY IN THE AUDIENCE

WOMEN'S VOICES

CHORUS

PROLOGUE

In front of the lowered curtain, THE DIRECTOR, *in evening dress, carrying a cane, emerges from the prompter's box*

⚊ *SCENE I* ⚊

THE DIRECTOR

So here I am back among you
Back with my dynamic company
I'm back on the stage
But sadly too I've come back
To a theatre that has no grandeur and no virtue
The same as used to deaden the long evenings before the war
It was a malicious harmful art-form
Displaying the sin not the redeemer

Then came the time the time for men
I have made war like all the men

It happened when I was in the artillery
On the northern front commanding my troop
One night when in the sky the eyes of all the stars
Twinkled up above like eyes of new-born babes
A thousand rockets from the trenches opposite
Suddenly roused the enemy's cannon

I remember it as though it were yesterday

I could hear them go up but not come down
When from the artillery observation post
The trumpeter on horseback came to tell us
That the sergeant who'd trained

163

The sights of his triangular alidade
On the distant glint of enemy cannon wanted us to know
That the range of those cannon was so immense
That you could no longer hear the shells burst
And all the gunners at their posts
Announced the stars were going out one by one
Then we heard loud cries from all the ranks

THEY'RE PUTTING OUT THE STARS WITH
    GUNFIRE

The stars were dying in the fine autumn sky
As memory dies in the brains
Of poor old men who try to remember
We were there dying the death of the stars
There at the murky front with its livid glints
We could only say despairing

THEY'VE EVEN MURDERED THE CONSTELLATIONS

But a loud voice through a megaphone
Whose horn poked out
Of God knows what command-post
The voice of the unknown captain who always saves us cried

IT'S HIGH TIME WE LIT THE STARS AGAIN

And the great French front let out a single cry

GO FOR THE RANGE-FINDERS

The gun crew hastened
The gun layers took aim
The gunners gunned
And the sublime stars lit up one by one
Our shells rekindled their eternal ardour

The enemy artillery fell silent dazzled
By the twinkling of all the stars

So that is the tale of all the stars

And from that night I too light one by one
The inner stars that were put out

So here I am back among you

My company don't be impatient

And my public wait but not impatiently

I bring you a play which aims to reform society
It's about children in the family
It's a domestic subject
And that's why it's given a homely treatment
The actors won't put on sinister voices
They'll quite simply appeal to your good sense
And they'll aim above all to amuse you
So you'll feel well-disposed and learn
From all the lessons in the play
And so that everywhere the ground will be sparkling
With the eyes of new-born babes
More of them than the twinkling stars

O Frenchmen hear the lesson of the war
Make children now you couples who forbore

I'm trying to bring a new spirit to the theatre
A spirit of joy ecstasy virtue
Instead of this pessimism aged at least a hundred
A ripe old age for a thing so tedious
The play was written for a traditional stage
For they wouldn't have built us a new one

A theatre in the round with two stages
One in the middle the other like a ring
Round the audience that would give us scope
To display our modern art to the full
As in life often linking unrelated
Sounds gestures colours shouts noise
Music dance acrobatics poetry painting
Choruses actions and multiple sets

Here you will see actions
Which add to the main plot and embellish it
Shifts of tone from pathos to burlesque
The plausible use of implausibilities
And actors collective or not
Who aren't just part of humanity
But of the whole universe
For theatre shouldn't be *trompe l'œil* art

It's right for the playwright to use
Every mirage at his disposal
Like Fata Morgana on Mount Jebal*
It's right for him to endow with speech
The crowd or inanimate objects
If he wants to
And for him to pay no heed to time
Nor space

His universe is his play
Within it he's God the creator
Displaying at will
Sounds gestures movements masses colours
Not just with the aim
Of photographing what we call a slice of life

But to bring out life itself in all its truthfulness
For the play should be an entire universe
With its creator
That's to say nature itself
And not merely
Show a small chunk
Of what's around us or what happened once

Forgive me my friends my company

Forgive me dear Public
I'm sorry I've spoken a bit too long
It's so long since I was with you

But still there stands a brazier out there
Where they shoot down the smoking stars
And the men who light them again are asking you
To raise yourselves up to those sublime flames
And catch fire too

O public
Be the unquenchable torch of the new flame

ACT I

The market-place in Zanzibar, morning. The set shows houses, a view of the port, and a number of items which should give the audience some idea of the game of zanzibar.* A megaphone shaped like a dice-shaker, decorated with dice, stands at the front of the stage. Stage right, the door of a house; stage left, a newspaper kiosk with a wealth of wares displayed and a dummy newspaper-seller with arms that move; on the kiosk hangs a mirror, facing the stage. At the back, a composite character who never speaks, representing THE PEOPLE OF ZANZIBAR, is already on-stage as the curtain rises. He is sitting on a bench. On his right is a table, and to hand are instruments which he will use for creating sound effects at appropriate moments: a revolver, a bagpipe,* a bass drum, an accordion, a drum, a thunder machine, sleigh-bells, castanets, a child's trumpet, and broken crockery. All the noises attributed to an instrument in the stage directions should be made by THE PEOPLE OF ZANZIBAR, and all speeches given as through a megaphone should be shouted at the audience

⚊ SCENE I ⚊

THE PEOPLE OF ZANZIBAR, THERESE

THERESE

Blue face, long blue dress decorated with painted monkeys and fruit. She enters as soon as the curtain is up, but even as the curtain is rising, she tries to shout down the orchestra

No Monsieur husband
You won't make me do what you want

Hissing sound

I'm a feminist and I don't accept men's authority

Hissing sound

Besides I want to do things my way
Men have been doing what they liked for long enough
What's more I want to go and fight the enemy
I fancy being a soldier one two one two
I want to make war (*Thunder*) and not make babies
No Monsieur husband you won't order me around any more

She bows three times, rump towards the audience

Through the megaphone

Just because you did the courting in Connecticut
Must I do the cooking in Zanzibar

HUSBAND'S VOICE

Belgian accent

Give me bacon fat I tell you give me bacon fat

Broken crockery

THERESE

Listen to him all he thinks about is sex

She has hysterics

But you haven't the faintest idea you idiot

Sneezes

After I've been a soldier I want to be an artist

Sneezes

Absolutely absolutely

Sneezes

And I want to be an MP a barrister a member of the
government

Two sneezes

A minister the president of the State

Sneezes

And I want to be a doctor curing bodies or brains
Poncing around Europe and America as I please
Making babies making meals no it's just too much

She cackles

I want to be a mathematician a philosopher a chemist
A page in a restaurant a little telegraph-boy
And that elderly chorus-girl with so much talent
I want to keep her in style for a year if I feel like it

Sneezes, cackles, then imitates the noise of a train

HUSBAND'S VOICE
Belgian accent

Give me bacon fat I tell you give me bacon fat

THERESE

Listen to him all he thinks about is sex

Short tune on the bagpipes

Go boil your trotters in their own juice*

Bass drum

But I think my beard's growing
My breasts are coming loose

*She gives a great cry and opens her blouse; her breasts pop out, one
blue, the other red, and as she lets them go they fly up, balloons on
the end of strings*

Fly away birds of my frailty
　　　　　Etcetera
How pretty feminine charms are
They're utterly delicious
Good enough to eat

　　She pulls the strings and makes the balloons bob about

But that's enough silliness
Don't let's go in for aerobatics
Being virtuous always pays off
After all vice is a dangerous thing
That's why it's better to sacrifice beauty
Which can give rise to sin
Let's get rid of my mammaries

　*She makes them explode with a cigarette-lighter, then pulls a
terrific face and cocks a double snook at the audience, and throws
them some balls she had in her bodice*

What does this mean
It's not just my beard growing it's my moustache too

*She strokes her beard and twirls the tips of her moustache which have
suddenly grown*

What the devil
I look like a cornfield ready for the combine harvester

Through the megaphone

I feel devilish virile
I'm a stallion
Top to bottom
I'm a bull

Without megaphone

I'll be a torero
But don't let's go on
Spreading the news of my future O hero
Put up your arms
And as for you husband less virile than me
Sound the alarms
As much as you want

> *Still cackling, she admires herself in the mirror on the newspaper kiosk*

⚓ SCENE II ⚓

THE PEOPLE OF ZANZIBAR, THERESE, THE HUSBAND

THE HUSBAND

Enters carrying a big bunch of flowers, sees that she isn't looking at him, and throws the flowers into the audience. From now on the Husband speaks without a Belgian accent

I tell you I want some bacon fat

THERESE

Go boil your trotters in their own juice

THE HUSBAND

During his speech THERESE*'s cacklings get louder and louder. He approaches her as though to slap her then with a laugh he says*

Oh but this isn't my wife Therese

    Pause. Then, through the megaphone, in a stern voice

Who's this lout wearing her clothes

He goes to examine her, then comes back. Through the megaphone

There's no doubt about it he's a murderer and he's killed her

    Without megaphone

Therese, where are you baby

    He reflects, head in hands, then legs apart, hands on hips

As for you monster of depravity disguised as Therese I'm going to kill you

    They fight and she wins

THERESE

You're right I'm not your wife any more

THE HUSBAND

Well I'm blowed

THERESE

Nevertheless I am Therese

THE HUSBAND

Well I'm blowed

THERESE

But Therese who isn't a woman now

THE HUSBAND

This is too much

THERESE

So now I've become a handsome guy

THE HUSBAND

That little detail had escaped me

THERESE

From now on I'll have a man's name
Tiresias

THE HUSBAND,
hands clasped

Adiousias*

Exit THERESE

☰ *SCENE III* ☰

THE PEOPLE OF ZANZIBAR, THE HUSBAND

TIRESIAS'S VOICE

I'm leaving home

THE HUSBAND

Adiousias

One after the other, she throws a chamber-pot, a basin, and a urinal out of the window. THE HUSBAND *picks up the chamber-pot*

174

The piano

> *He picks up the urinal*

The violin

> *He picks up the basin*

The butter-dish this is getting serious

⚎ SCENE IV ⚎

THE SAME, TIRESIAS, LACOUF, PRESTO

Enter TIRESIAS *with clothes, a rope, miscellaneous objects. She throws them aside and flings herself on the Husband. During the Husband's last speech* PRESTO *and* LACOUF, *armed with Brownings made of cardboard, have solemnly emerged from under the stage and are advancing through the audience, while* TIRESIAS, *overpowering her husband, removes his trousers, undresses herself, puts her skirt on him and ties him up, puts on his trousers, cuts off her hair, and puts on a top hat. The action goes on till the first shot is heard.*

PRESTO

Playing zanzibar with you Lacouf old fellow I've lost
Everything I could possibly lose

LACOUF

Monsieur Presto I haven't won a thing

And anyway it's nothing to do with Zanzibar you're in
   Paris

PRESTO

In Zanzibar

LACOUF

In Paris

PRESTO

This is too much
After ten years of friendship
And all the dreadful things I've always said about you

LACOUF

Too bad did I ask for publicity you're in Paris

PRESTO

In Zanzibar I've lost everything that proves it

LACOUF

Monsieur Presto we must have a fight

PRESTO

Yes we must

*Gravely, they climb onto the stage and take up positions at the back,
facing each other*

LACOUF

On equal terms

PRESTO

As you please
In this life you never know what's going to hit you

They aim at each other. THE PEOPLE OF ZANZIBAR *fires two revolver shots and they fall*

TIRESIAS,

who is now ready, shudders at the sound and cries

Beloved freedom I've won you at last
But first let me buy a paper
To find out what's just happened

She buys a paper and reads it; meanwhile The People of Zanzibar places a placard on each side of the stage:

PLACARD FOR PRESTO

FIRST HE LOST AT ZANZIBAR
NOW MONSIEUR PRESTO'S LOST HIS BET
PARIS IS WHERE THIS IS SET

PLACARD FOR LACOUF

MONSIEUR LACOUF'S WON NOTHING
THE SCENE IS SET IN ZANZIBAR
AS THE SEINE IS SET IN PARIS

As soon as THE PEOPLE OF ZANZIBAR *is back in his place,* PRESTO *and* LACOUF *stand up,* THE PEOPLE OF ZANZIBAR *fires a shot from his revolver, and* THE DUELLISTS *fall down again.* TIRESIAS *throws aside the paper in surprise*

Through the megaphone

And now the universe will be mine
Women will be mine the government will be mine
I'm going to make myself a local councillor
But I hear noises

Perhaps I'd better go away

Exit, cackling, while THE HUSBAND *imitates the noise of a train in motion*

♒ *SCENE V* ♒

THE PEOPLE OF ZANZIBAR, THE HUSBAND, THE POLICEMAN

THE POLICEMAN

Whilst THE PEOPLE OF ZANZIBAR *plays the accordion,* THE POLICEMAN *on horseback prances about, drags one of the corpses into the wings so that only his feet are visible, rides round the stage, does the same with the other corpse, rides round the stage again, and notices* THE HUSBAND *tied up, front of stage*

It stinks of crime round here.

THE HUSBAND

Ah! since at last we have a representative
Of Zanzibarian authority
I'll address him
Excuse me Monsieur if you have business with me
Be so good as to take
My military papers out of my left-hand pocket

THE POLICEMAN,
through the megaphone

What a pretty girl

178

Without megaphone

Tell me my dear young lady
Who has treated you so abominably

THE HUSBAND,
aside

He thinks I'm a girl

To the Policeman

If it's marriage you're after

THE POLICEMAN *lays his hand on his heart*

Untie me for a start

THE POLICEMAN *unties him, tickling him as he does so, they both laugh, and* THE POLICEMAN *keeps repeating* What a pretty girl

⚊ *SCENE VI* ⚊

THE SAME, PRESTO, LACOUF

As soon as THE POLICEMAN *starts to untie the Husband,* PRESTO *and* LACOUF *re-enter, back to where they were standing when they fell*

PRESTO

I'm getting tired of being dead
To think that some people
Think it's more honourable to be dead than alive

LACOUF

Now you see you weren't in Zanzibar

PRESTO

And yet one would wish to live there
But I'm disgusted at us for fighting a duel
There's no doubt that people view death
With too kindly an eye

LACOUF

What do you expect people have too good an opinion
Of humanity and its leavings
Does the excrement of jewellers
Contain pearls and diamonds

PRESTO

Stranger things have happened

LACOUF

In short Monsieur Presto
You've no luck with bets
You can see quite clearly you were in Paris

PRESTO

In Zanzibar

LACOUF

Take aim

PRESTO

Fire

THE PEOPLE OF ZANZIBAR *fires a shot from the revolver and they fall.* THE POLICEMAN *finishes untying the Husband*

THE POLICEMAN

You're under arrest

PRESTO *and* LACOUF *run away, opposite sides from where they re-entered. Accordion*

⚎ *SCENE VII* ⚎

THE PEOPLE OF ZANZIBAR, THE POLICEMAN,
THE HUSBAND, *dressed as a woman*

THE POLICEMAN

The local duellists
Won't stop me telling you that I find you
Lovely to touch like a ball you can squeeze

THE HUSBAND

Sneeze

Broken crockery

THE POLICEMAN

A cold you're exquisite you

THE HUSBAND

Itchoo

Drums. THE HUSBAND *raises his skirt which is hampering him*

THE POLICEMAN

Loose woman

181

He winks

But who cares if she's a pretty girl

THE HUSBAND

By god he's right
Since my wife is a man
It's right for me to be a woman

Bashfully, to the Policeman

I'm a respectable wife-monsieur
My wife's a man-madame
She's gone off with the piano the violin the butter-dish
She's a soldier a minister a phy-shit-ian

THE POLICEMAN

Phy-tits-ian*

THE HUSBAND

She's exploded *them* so she's more of a phy-shit-ian

THE POLICEMAN

She's more of a phy-swan-song*
Ah! How they sing when they're dying*
Listen

Sad tune on the bagpipes

THE HUSBAND

It's all about the art of healing men
The music will take care of that
As well as any other panacea

THE POLICEMAN

Come along now no rough stuff

THE HUSBAND

I refuse to continue with this conversation

Through the megaphone

Where's my wife

WOMEN'S VOICES
in the wings

Hurrah for Tiresias
No more babies no more babies

Thunder, bass drum. THE HUSBAND *makes a face at the audience and cups his hand round his ear, while* THE POLICEMAN, *taking a pipe from his pocket, offers it to him. Sleigh bells*

THE POLICEMAN

Hey! Shepherdess come smoke your pipe
And I will play my pipes for you

THE HUSBAND

Yet in seven years the Baker's Wife
Will shed her skin for one that's new

THE HUSBAND

Every seven years what a life

THE PEOPLE OF ZANZIBAR *hangs up a noticeboard with these words on it. It should be left in place:*

HEY! SHEPHERDESS COME SMOKE YOUR PIPE
AND I WILL PLAY MY PIPES FOR YOU
YET IN SEVEN YEARS THE BAKER'S WIFE

WILL SHED HER SKIN FOR ONE THAT'S NEW
EVERY SEVEN YEARS WHAT A LIFE

THE POLICEMAN

Mademoiselle or Madame I love you true
I do
And I would like to marry you

THE HUSBAND

A-tishoo
But can't you see I'm only a man

THE POLICEMAN

Nevertheless I could marry you
By special licence

THE HUSBAND

Rubbish
You'd do better to father babies

THE POLICEMAN

Well really!

MEN'S VOICES
in the wings

Hurrah for Tiresias
Hurrah for Tiresias the general
Hurrah for Tiresias the Member of Parliament

The accordion plays a military march

WOMEN'S VOICES
in the wings

No more babies No more babies

≈ *SCENE VIII* ≈

THE SAME, THE KIOSK

THE KIOSK, *with its shopkeeper's arm in motion, moves slowly to the other side of the stage*

THE HUSBAND

Great representative of high authority
You hear what has been said I feel with clarity
Women in Zanzibar demand representation
They've utterly renounced all love and procreation
No more babies no more is their eternal cry
To people Zanzibar it's elephants you should try
And snakes flies ostriches and monkeys in the trees
While woman will be sterile as a hive of bees
Bees at least make wax and cells with honey fill
But women would be neuters before heaven still
My dear Monsieur O hear the urgent tale I tell

Through the megaphone

Zanzibar needs its babies (*Without the megaphone*) you must
   go and yell
At the street corners on the boulevards
We must make children now in Zanzibar
Women won't have them Too bad Let men do it
Yes really and I mean to get down to it
I'm not pretending

THE POLICEMAN AND THE KIOSK

You

THE KIOSK,
through the megaphone which THE HUSBAND *hands to her*

She's spinning a yarn
Which must be heard not just in Zanzibar
You who weep as you watch the play
Pray that the children win the day
Witness the ardour beyond belief
Arising from a change of sex

THE HUSBAND

I will have offspring though I have no wife
To see how it is done come back to me tonight

THE POLICEMAN

You will have offspring though you have no wife
To see how it is done I will come back tonight
To keep me waiting would be quite absurd
I will return I take you at your word

THE KIOSK

That copper there's a gormless one
To govern over Zanzibar
He'd rather be in club or bar
Enjoying himself and having fun
Than populating Zanzibar

⚜ *SCENE IX* ⚜

THE SAME, PRESTO

PRESTO,
tickling the Husband

How can we give such beings a name
Though physically she's just the same
To call her man's not playing the game

THE POLICEMAN

You will have offspring though you have no wife
To see how it is done I will come back tonight

THE HUSBAND

I will have offspring though I have no wife
To see how it is done come back to me tonight

ALL,
in chorus

They dance, THE HUSBAND *and* THE POLICEMAN *with each other,* PRESTO *and* THE KIOSK *with each other, and sometimes changing partners.* THE PEOPLE OF ZANZIBAR *dances alone playing his accordion*

Hey! Shepherdess come smoke your pipe
And I will play my pipes for you
Yet in seven years the Baker's Wife
Will shed her skin for one that's new
Every seven years what a life

CURTAIN

ACT II

The same place, the same day, sunset. The same decor, plus numerous cradles full of new-born infants. An empty cradle stands beside an enormous ink-bottle, a gigantic pot of glue, an outsize pen, and a pair of giant scissors

[CHORUS]*

⚊ SCENE I ⚊

THE PEOPLE OF ZANZIBAR, THE HUSBAND

THE HUSBAND

He is carrying a baby on each arm. Continual wailing of infants onstage, in the wings and in the auditorium throughout the scene, ad libitum. The stage directions merely indicate when they increase in volume

Ah! The joys of fatherhood are simply wild
40,049 infants in a single day
My happiness is complete
Shut up shut up

> *Wailing of infants from the back of the stage*

A happy family life
No wife to support

> *He drops the infants*

Shut up

> *Wailing of infants from the left side of the auditorium*

Isn't modern music fantastic
Almost as fantastic as stage sets by modern painters
Who flourish far from the Barbarians
Of Zanzibar
Who needs the Paris Theatre or the Russian Ballet*
Shut up shut up

*Wailing of infants from the right side of the auditorium. Sleigh
bells*

Although it's discipline they need
I'd best be slow and dozy
I'll get them bicycles instead
And all these virtuosi
With talent to spare
Will give concerts*
In the open air

Gradually the infants quieten down. He claps

Bravo bravo bravo

Knocking

Come in

⚊ *SCENE II* ⚊

THE SAME, THE PARISIAN JOURNALIST

THE JOURNALIST

*His face is blank, except for the mouth. He dances in.
Accordion*

Hands up
How do you do Monsieur Husband
I'm a newspaper correspondent from Paris

THE HUSBAND

From Paris
Pleased to meet you

THE JOURNALIST
dances round the stage

The newspapers in Paris (*Through the megaphone*) a town in
America

Without the megaphone

Hurrah

Pistol-shot, THE JOURNALIST *unfurls an American flag*

Carry the story that you have found
A way for men
To bear children

THE JOURNALIST *folds up the flag and makes it into a belt*

THE HUSBAND

That's the truth

THE JOURNALIST

So how come

THE HUSBAND

Will-power Monsieur can achieve anything

THE JOURNALIST

Are they black or like normal people

THE HUSBAND

That depends on where you're standing

Castanets

THE JOURNALIST

I expect you're well-off

He dances around

THE HUSBAND

Not at all

THE JOURNALIST

How are you going to bring them up?

THE HUSBAND

When I've done with bottle feeds
I hope they'll cater for my needs

THE JOURNALIST

So you're like a kind of daughter-father
Is there a maternalized paternal instinct in you

THE HUSBAND

No my dear Monsieur self-interest is the clue
A child is a family's pride
And family wealth is nothing by his side

THE JOURNALIST *takes notes*

Look at this little mite a-sleeping in his crib

The baby cries. THE JOURNALIST *tiptoes over to look at him*

Arthur's his name. He's already made
A fortune with exclusive rights in curdled milk

Child's trumpet

THE JOURNALIST

He's forward for his age

THE HUSBAND

This one Joseph (*The baby cries*) he's a novelist

THE JOURNALIST *goes and looks at Joseph*

His last novel sold 600,000 copies
Allow me to present you with one

Takes down a big poster made like a book with leaves and on the front leaf we can read the words:

WHAT LUCK!

A NOVEL

THE HUSBAND

Read it at your leisure

THE JOURNALIST *lies down,* THE HUSBAND *turns the other pages showing the audience these words, one word per page:*

A LADY WHOSE NAME WAS CRAPP*

THE JOURNALIST
gets up and speaks through the megaphone

A lady whose name was Crapp

Through the megaphone he laughs on the four vowel-sounds:
a, e, i, o

THE HUSBAND

Nevertheless there is a refinement of expression here

THE JOURNALIST,
not through the megaphone

Ha! Ha! Ha! Ha!

THE HUSBAND

It shows a precociousness

THE JOURNALIST

Hee! Hee!

THE HUSBAND

Which is way out of the ordinary

THE JOURNALIST

Hands up

THE HUSBAND

Anyway such as it is
The novel has made me
Nearly 200,000 francs
Plus a literary prize
Consisting of 20 crates of dynamite

THE JOURNALIST,
exiting backwards

Goodbye

THE HUSBAND

Don't be scared they're in my safe deposit at the bank

THE JOURNALIST

All right
Don't you have any daughters

THE HUSBAND

Yes indeed this one she's divorced

She cries. THE JOURNALIST *goes to look at her*

From the potato king
She gets 100,000 dollars alimony
And this one (*she cries*) the most creative artist in
    Zanzibar

THE JOURNALIST *practises shadow-boxing*

Recites lovely verses on dull evenings
Every year with her passion and her style she makes as
    much
As a poet earns in fifty thousand years

THE JOURNALIST

Congratulations my dear chap
But you've got dust
On your dust-coat

THE HUSBAND *smiles as if to thank* THE JOURNALIST *who
holds a speck of dust in his hand*

Since you're so rich lend me a few pence

THE HUSBAND

Put that dust back

All the children cry. THE HUSBAND *drives the Journalist away,
kicking him. Exit* THE JOURNALIST *dancing*

⚊ *SCENE III* ⚊

THE PEOPLE OF ZANZIBAR, THE HUSBAND

THE HUSBAND

Well yes it's simple as a periscope
The more children I have
The richer I'll be and the better I'll live
They say the codfish lays enough eggs in a day
To feed the entire world for a whole year
On fish soup and aioli
When they're hatched
Isn't it great to have a big family
Who are those idiotic economists
Who made us believe that children
Spell poverty
When it's just the opposite
Has anyone ever heard of a codfish starving to death
That's why I'll go on having children
Let's start by having a journalist
So then I'll know everything
I'll guess the extras
And invent the rest

He begins to tear up newspapers with his teeth and hands, thrashing about. His movements should be very rapid

He must be capable of every chore
Able to write for every party

He puts the torn-up newspapers in the empty cradle

What a fine journalist he'll be

Factual reports in-depth articles
Et cetera
He needs a blood supply from the inkwell

> *He takes a bottle of ink and pours it into the cradle*

He needs a spine

> *He puts an enormous pen into the cradle*

Brains so he doesn't have to think

> *He tips a pot of glue into the cradle*

A tongue—all the better for drivelling

> *He puts some scissors into the cradle*

Lastly, he's got to have a song to sing
Come on, sing now

> *Thunder*

≈ SCENE IV ≈

THE SAME, THE SON

THE HUSBAND *repeats: 'one, two!' until the end of the Son's
speech. This scene is played very fast*

THE SON
stands up in his cradle

My dear Papa you want to fish
For scandals then the dirt I'll dish
Just dole me out some pocket money
The printing presses are like trees
Leaf upon leaf flaps in the breeze

The papers have grown they're ready to pick
To make a salad to feed the kids
You'd better give me five hundred francs
To keep my mouth shut 'bout your affairs
If not I'll blab and I'll be frank
Papa and sibs will not be spared
I'll write about how the wife you took
Was already expecting triplets; what's more
To make big trouble I'll say you're a crook
You steal kill wheel and deal you bore

THE HUSBAND

Bravo the brilliant blackmailer

THE SON *climbs out of the cradle*

THE SON

My dear parents two in one
If you want to know last night's news
Here goes
A vast fire destroyed Niagara Falls

THE HUSBAND

Too bad

THE SON

The handsome builder Alcindor
Dressed like a soldier in disguise
Through the night played on his horn
To a roomful of murderers harmonized
I dare say he played till morn

THE HUSBAND

Let's hope it didn't happen here

THE SON

But the Princess of Bergamo
Is soon to marry a lady who
She got to know in the métro

Castanets

THE HUSBAND

What do I care do I know these people
I want to hear good news about my friends

THE SON

rocks the cradle

And now here is the latest news
Brought to you fresh from Montrouge*
Picasso's invented a picture able
To move on its own just like this cradle

THE HUSBAND

He's such a virtuoso
My good friend Picasso*
O my son
Leave it for another time I now know
Quite enough
About what happened yesterday

THE SON

I'm going off to invent what's happening tomorrow

THE HUSBAND

Bon voyage

Exit THE SON

≈ *SCENE V* ≈

THE PEOPLE OF ZANZIBAR, THE HUSBAND

THE HUSBAND

That one's good for nothing
I've a good mind to cut him out of my will

Posters showing telegraphed messages appear:

OTTAWA

MAJOR FIRE JCB ESTABLISHMENTS STOP
20,000 PROSE POEMS CONSUMED STOP PRESIDENT
SENDS CONDOLENCES

ROME

H.NR.M.T.SS. DIRECTOR VILLA MEDICI COMPLETES
PORTRAIT SS

AVIGNON

TOP ARTIST G..RG.S BRAQUE INVENTS METHOD
INTENSIVE CULTURE OF PAINTBRUSHES

VANCOUVER TRANSMISSION DELAYED

MONSIEUR LEAUT..D'S DOGS ON STRIKE*

THE HUSBAND

Enough enough I say
What a dumb idea to make the Press my friend
They just won't go away
They bother me all day
It's damn well got to end

Through the megaphone

Hallo hallo Mademoiselle
Cancel my subscription to the phone
I want to un-telephone

Without the megaphone

Change of plan no more useless mouths
I must cut down cut down
And first I must make my next child a tailor
Then I can look well-dressed when I go out
And as I'm quite a decent looking chap
Plenty pretty girls will fancy me

▲▲▲ *SCENE VI* ▲▲▲

THE SAME, THE POLICEMAN

THE POLICEMAN

I hear you're going great guns
You've kept your word
40,050 children in one day
You're rocking the boat

THE HUSBAND

I'm coining it in

THE POLICEMAN

But the population of Zanzibar
Reduced to starvation by the excess of mouths to feed
Is in danger of dying of hunger

THE HUSBAND

Issue them with cards—that'll do the trick

THE POLICEMAN

Where does one obtain them

THE HUSBAND

From the lady who reads cards

THE POLICEMAN

Thanks a million

THE HUSBAND

Well since you want to plan for the future

⚞ *SCENE VII* ⚞

THE SAME, THE FORTUNE-TELLER

Enter FORTUNE-TELLER *at the back of the auditorium. Electrical light-effects round her head*

THE FORTUNE-TELLER

Citizens of Zanzibar so pure and chaste I am here

THE HUSBAND

Another caller
I'm not at home to anyone

THE FORTUNE-TELLER

I thought you'd all be pleased
To have your fortunes told

THE POLICEMAN

You are well aware Madame
That you are exercising an illegal profession
It's astonishing what folks will do
To get out of doing an honest day's work

THE HUSBAND,

to the Policeman

No hanky-panky in my house please

THE FORTUNE-TELLER,

to a member of the audience

In the near future you Monsieur
Will be brought to bed of three sets of twins

THE HUSBAND

What competition already

A LADY

(*a member of the audience*)

Madame Fortune-Teller
I think he's two-timing me

Sound of breaking dishes

THE FORTUNE-TELLER

Pop him in the hay-box

She climbs onto the stage, sound of children crying, accordion playing

Well I never an incubator

THE HUSBAND

Are you the barber short back and sides please

THE FORTUNE-TELLER

The young girls of New York
Pick greengages to eat

All they like is ham from York
That's why they are so sweet

THE HUSBAND

Parisiennes are nice
Much nicer than the rest
If pussies all love mice
We love your pussies best

THE FORTUNE-TELLER

He means your puss-onalities

ALL
(*in chorus*)

So sing from morn till night
And scratch wherever you itch
Feel free to go for black or white
It can be fun to switch
Just mind you get it right
Just mind you get it right

THE FORTUNE-TELLER

Pure and chaste citizens of Zanzibar
No longer willing to give birth to infants
Know now that fame and fortune are
With pineapple groves and elephants
Reserved by right
Or will be all right
For those who've earned them by producing infants

All the children start crying on stage and in the auditorium. THE
FORTUNE-TELLER *tells fortunes with cards which fall from
above. Then the children fall quiet*

You who are so fertile

THE HUSBAND and THE POLICEMAN

Fertile fertile

THE FORTUNE-TELLER,
to the Husband

You will be a millionaire ten times over

THE HUSBAND *falls to the ground in a sitting position*

THE FORTUNE-TELLER,
to the Policeman

You who don't produce children
You will die in abject poverty

THE POLICEMAN

This is an insult
I arrest you in the name of Zanzibar

THE FORTUNE-TELLER

Aren't you ashamed to lay hands on a woman

She claws him and strangles him. THE HUSBAND *hands her a pipe*

THE HUSBAND

Hey! Shepherdess come smoke your pipe
And I will play my pipes for you
Yet in seven years the Baker's Wife
Will shed her skin for one that's new

THE FORTUNE-TELLER

Every seven years what a life

THE HUSBAND

Meanwhile I'm taking you down to the police station
You murderess

THERESE,
ripping off her tawdry fortune-teller's costume

Don't you recognize me husband dear

THE HUSBAND

Therese or should I say Tiresias

THE POLICEMAN *comes back to life*

THERESE

Tiresias is at present officially
Commander-in-chief of the Army MP Lord Mayor
But keep your hair on
I've got a removal van to bring back
The piano the violin the butter-dish
And also three influential ladies who've become my mistresses

THE POLICEMAN

Thanks for bearing me in mind

THE HUSBAND

Monsieur General Monsieur MP
I beg your pardon I mean Therese
You're as flat-chested as a bedbug

THERESE

Too bad let's go pick strawberries
And flowers from the banana tree

205

Go hunting like Zanzibarese
For elephants so come with me
Reign o'er the heart of your Therese

HUSBAND

Therese

THERESE

They're one and the same the throne the tomb
We need to love or else succumb
Before this curtain down does come

THE HUSBAND

Dear Therese you can't remain
Flat-chested like a bedbug

He fetches a bunch of balloons and a basket of balls from the house

Here are fresh supplies

THERESE

You and I managed OK without them
Let's just carry on

THE HUSBAND

You're right let's not complicate our lives
Let's go and have our soup instead

THERESE
Lets loose the balloons and throws the balls at the audience

Fly away birds of my weakness
Go and feed all the babies
Of the repopulation

ALL

(*in chorus*)

THE PEOPLE OF ZANZIBAR *dances, rattling bells*

So sing from morn till night
And scratch wherever you itch
Feel free to go for black or white
It can be fun to switch
Just mind you get it right

CURTAIN

EXPLANATORY NOTES

THE BLIND

1 *Charles Van Lerberghe*: an old schoolfriend of Maeterlinck's, and a minor literary figure in his own right.

2 *THE PRIEST*: this character neither speaks nor moves throughout the play. Normally an effigy is used.

30 *the flowers of the dead*: asphodels are native flowers of Greece. Homer describes them growing in the Elysian fields, where the dead gathered. The fact that Maeterlinck has them growing, however limply, in this icy forest demonstrates how little he cared for verisimilitude and authentic detail.

33 *A big dog*: Maeterlinck was against using a real animal here. In the original production, he was overruled by the director. But the dog has too difficult a part to play for a canine actor, and he reduced the audience to mirth by his visible reluctance to lead the blind man to the body of the priest.

UBU THE KING

51 *Marcel Schwob*: Jarry's close friend and first publisher.

noddle: Jarry uses the French word *poire*, literally 'pear'. In his own original illustrations, he draws Ubu pear-shaped.

52 *CHARACTERS*: Jarry put all his powers of invention into these names, which gradually evolved over the years. For the name UBU, see the Introduction. For CAPTAIN BRUBBISH, see Translator's Note. For QUEEN ROSEMONDE, see Introduction. BUGGERLAS parodies and undermines the grand Polish names of his father and brothers. For the names of the 'PILLODINS', see Introduction. 'Pillodin' itself was a problem to translate. In French the Pillodins are *Palotins*, clearly a corruption of *paladins* with a hint of *salopins* ('guttersnipes'). The first syllable of 'Palotins' has a very specific Ubuesque meaning: the *pal* is a phallic rod used for impaling Ubu's victims. My 'Pillodins' attempts to suggest 'paladins' while subverting the word by incorporating a suggestion of 'pillock' and 'pillow'. For THE ENTIRE RUSSIAN AND

POLISH ARMIES, see Introduction. To render THE HORSE OF THE PHYNANCES and the other horses Jarry hung amateurish cardboard horses' heads round the actors' necks.

55 *By the wick of my candle*: Ubu's favourite oath, 'de par ma chandelle verte', which literally means 'by my green candle', is in part a reminder of the chemistry teacher Hébert and his equipment (see Introduction). In *Ubu Cuckold* there is the following stage direction: 'Meanwhile Père Ubu lights his green candle, a hydrogen flame in sulphur vapour, which, constructed according to the principle of the philosophical Organ, emits a continuous fluting sound.' 'Vert' has a second, old-fashioned, meaning of 'alive' or even 'randy', not 'green' at all. That 'vert' is meant to have an archaic flavour here is clear from the beginning of the oath, 'de par', which traditionally preceded a royal proclamation. Ubu, in grand and old-fashioned language, is alluding obscenely to his 'living candle'. My version, 'by the wick of my candle', renders the phallic innuendo and (I hope) brings to mind the Yorkshire word *wick*, meaning 'alive'.

56 *a prosperous gentleman*: the first of a number of quotations from *Macbeth*, incorporated into the translation as Shakespeare's play was such a blatant source of inspiration to Jarry.

68 *Sandomierz*: genuine, like most of the other Polish names in the play.

70 *unseam him . . . to the chaps*: from *Macbeth*, I. ii.

80 *he splits his belly*: typically, Ubu emerges unscathed after this horrific injury, which is never mentioned again.

109 *There! There's the gold, amongst the bones of kings*: the first of three iambic pentameters included here to imitate Jarry's alexandrines (see Note on the Translation).

123 *Sanctificetur nomen tuum*: Ubu starts reciting a paternoster, the Latin Lord's Prayer.

125 *the wooden horse*: in Homer's *Iliad* Greek soldiers, besieging Troy, hid inside a wooden horse. The Trojans innocently wheeled the horse inside their city walls and were thus defeated.

131 *right by my side*: the beginning of Mère Ubu's verse would be recognizable to a French audience as a quotation from Racine's *Andromaque* (*Andromache*); but in Racine's play, the lines are spoken by Orestes, who has gone tragically mad, his reason lost because of the horror of his plight, and who is seeing visions of the Furies: it is they whom he has 'spied'.

136 *Omnis a Deo scientia*: Ubu correctly translates, but wrongly construes, this phrase. The thought is biblical (Prov. 2: 6, Wisd. 7: 16, Sir. 11: 15), but the precise wording is not; it probably passed for proverbial.

146 *France...Mondragon...Elsinore...Spain*: this geographical confusion emphasizes the fact that Jarry wanted the play to be set in the land of 'Nowhere'. However, some of the places have a certain appropriateness: Ubu was at one time King of Aragon in Spain, and Elsinore reminds us that the plot is partly a parody of Shakespeare.

in Paris: *Ubu Bound* is indeed set in Paris.

THE MAMMARIES OF TIRESIAS

153 *fourteen years before*: most critics agree that this is unlikely. The subject of repopulation was topical after the war, and besides, Apollinaire had several times remarked that he had never written a play. It is thought that he made this claim partly because he feared accusations of plagiarism—his play appeared very soon after Cocteau's *Parade*—and partly because he was afraid his play would seem naïve and immature.

known to us simply as 'plays': see Introduction for a description of nineteenth-century theatre.

'surrealist': see Introduction for discussion of this term.

M. Victor Basch: in his article, published in *Le Pays*, 15 July 1917, Basch describes the play as an anti-feminist satire.

Scribe: Eugène Scribe (1791–1861), dramatist and librettist.

Nivelle de la Chaussée: Pierre-Claude Nivelle de la Chaussée (1692–1754), dramatist.

154 *the problem of repopulation*: see Introduction.

Farce of Master Pierre Pathelin: a hilarious anonymous farce of the fifteenth century.

155 *Delphic oracle*: the most famous oracle of ancient Greece—it was on a spot near the temple of Apollo and supposed to be the centre of the earth, and the prophecies were delivered by a priestess, the Pythia.

M. Deffoux: his article appeared in *La Caravane*, 20 July 1917.

156 *certain items...neo-Malthusians*: condoms. The English economist Thomas Robert Malthus (1766–1834) warned against the population explosion, and advocated sexual continence.

159 *LOUISE MARION*: these poems were dedicated by Apollinaire to members of the original cast. Louise Marion played Therese, Marcel Herrand the husband, Yeta Daesslé several parts including Lacouf, the moving kiosk, and the journalist, Juliette Norville the Policeman, and Howard (whose full name is not given) the People of Zanzibar.

166 *Fata Morgana on Mount Jebal*: Fata Morgana is a mirage effect in which objects seen from a distance seem vertically elongated. Mount Jebal is my guess (Apollinaire wrote 'mont Gibel'). The Jebala Mountains are a mountain range in Morocco—but there are many mountains with this name in the Middle East, as *jebal* or *djebel* is the Arabic word for 'mountain'.

168 *the game of zanzibar*: a game of chance, played with two or three dice and a dice-box.
bagpipe: Apollinaire has *une musette*, a kind of rustic bagpipe.

170 *in their own juice*: in the original, she tells him to cook his feet *à la Sainte-Ménéhould*, a method, evolved in the Argonne and much appreciated by gourmets, of cooking pig's trotters. To be really authentic, they should be boiled till the bones are soft, then breaded and fried or grilled.

174 *Adiousias*: the husband adapts his adieu to make it rhyme with 'Tiresias'.

182 *phy-shit-ian . . . phy-tits-ian*: Apollinaire writes *merdecin* instead of *médecin* ('a doctor'): *merde* means 'shit'. The policeman ripostes with *mère des seins*, 'mother of tits'.
phy-swan-song: continuing the pun on *médecin* (see previous note), the original has *mère des cygnes*—'mother of swans'.
How they sing when they're dying: swans were once believed to break into song as they died. The legend was that Zeus, grateful for the swan disguise which enabled him to seduce Leda, granted them this privilege.

188 [*CHORUS*]: in the original production, three choirs on the left, right, and back of the stage sing to words taken from Act I:
1. You who weep as you watch the play | Pray that the children win the day | Witness the ardour beyond belief | Arising from a change of sex
2. That copper there's a gormless one | To govern over Zanzibar | He'd rather be in club or bar | Enjoying himself and having fun | Than populating Zanzibar
3. How can we give such beings a name | Though physically she's just the same | To call her man's not playing the game

Explanatory Notes

189 *Russian Ballet*: from 1908 till after Apollinaire's death, Diaghilev's Ballets russes performed regularly in Paris. They were much admired by Apollinaire and his artist friends.

concerts: should be pronounced 'consair', à la française.

192 *CRAPP*: Apollinaire wrote *Cambron*, a clear reminiscence of *Cambronne*. Cambronne was one of Napoleon's generals. Ordered to surrender at Waterloo, the story has it that he replied *merde*, literally 'crap', to indicate his intention to disobey. *Merde* has since been known as 'Le mot de Cambronne'.

198 *Montrouge*: a suburb of Paris.

Picasso: actually one of Apollinaire's best friends, till he let him down by disowning him when they were both arrested in connection with the theft of the *Mona Lisa* (see Chronology).

199 *MAJOR FIRE . . . DOGS ON STRIKE*: the disguised names are those of Apollinaire's friends, the writers Max Jacob and Paul Léautaud and the painters Henri Matisse and Georges Braque. SS is unidentified. The Villa Medici, one of the great Roman Renaissance villas, has a fine collection of paintings and sculpture.